REPUBLIC PICTURES SERIAL LOCATIONS

by
Jerry L. Schneider

A CP Book
First Edition
March 2025

Published by
CP Books

For a list of our books, please visit our web site at
www.CPEntBooks.com

Copyright © 2025 Jerry L. Schneider.

isbn 979-8-9900581-2-5

All rights reserved. No part of this book may be reproduced or transmitted in any form by any means, electronic, mechanical, photocopying, recording, or by any information source and retrieval system now known or to be invented, without prior written permission of the publisher, except for the quoting of brief passages in connection with a review of this book.

CP Entertainment Books
www.CPEntBooks.com

Introduction

This book was in the process of image gathering from the Republic Pictures serials when I discovered that a book had been published by McFarland which was devoted to serial locations for a select number of serials. I ordered the book and read it, meanwhile having put my book on hold. After finding that the book lacked a lot on the different locations for each serial and also included several mistakes as to location, I decided to finish my book. Here is the final product.

CONTENTS

A Brief History of Republic Studio and Republic Pictures	i
A Brief Look at the Backlot Locations	iii
Darkest Africa	1
Undersea Kingdom	6
The Vigilantes Are Coming	11
Robinson Crusoe of Clipper Island	16
Dick Tracy	21
The Painted Stallion	28
SOS Coast Guard	34
Zorro Rides Again	44
The Lone Ranger	55
The Fighting Devil Dogs	60
Dick Tracy Returns	64
Hawk of the Wilderness	75
The Lone Ranger Rides Again	83
Daredevils of the Red Circle	91
Dick Tracy's G-Men	98
Zorro's Fighting Legion	111
Drums of Fu Manchu	117
Adventures of Red Ryder	124
King of the Royal Mounted	130
Mysterious Doctor Satan	136
Adventures of Captain Marvel	146
Jungle Girl	157
King of the Texas Rangers	164
Dick Tracy vs. Crime, Inc.	175
Spy Smasher	184
Perils of Nyoka	192
King of the Mounties	197

G-Men versus Black Dragon	202
Daredevils of the West	206
Secret Service in Darkest Africa	211
The Masked Marvel	216
Captain America	222
The Tiger Woman	227
Haunted Harbor	231
Zorro's Black Whip	237
Manhunt of Mystery Island	241
Federal Operator 99	248
The Purple Monster Strikes	254
The Phantom Rider	259
King of the Forest Rangers	264
Daughter of Don Q	267
The Crimson Ghost	271
Son of Zorro	275
Jesse James Rides Again	279
The Black Widow	283
G-Men Never Forget	290
Dangers of the Canadian Mounted	294
Adventures of Frank and Jesse James	299
Federal Agents vs Underworld Inc	302
Ghost of Zorro	306
King of the Rocket Men	309
The James Brothers of Missouri	314
Radar Patrol vs Spy King	319
The Invisible Monster	324
Desperadoes of the West	330
Flying Disc Man From Mars	334
Don Daredevil Rides Again	342
Government Agents vs Phantom Legion	346

Radar Men From the Moon	356
Zombies of the Stratosphere	367
Jungle Drums of Africa	379
Canadian Mounties vs Atomic Invaders	385
Trader Tom of the China Seas	389
Man with the Steel Whip	395
Panther Girl of the Kongo	399
King of the Carnival	404
Commando Cody	410

A BRIEF HISTORY OF REPUBLIC STUDIO AND REPUBLIC PICTURES

The history of Republic Pictures was reminiscent to the founding of Universal Pictures. However, the history of Republic Studios predates the forming of Republic Pictures.

On May 5, 1927, the incorporation papers for the Central Motion Picture District, Inc., were filed with the state of California (this would be the beginning of the pre-history of the studio). Among the directors of the company were Milton E. Hoffman, Gilbert H. Beesemeyer, Herman A. Zuber, Marlowe E. Merrick, Arthur M. Hazel, James R. Canterbury, Jr., and H. H. Merrick. On July 7, 1927, Charles H. Christie became chairman of the board. The company, with $3 million in capital, according to trade magazine and newspaper accounts, began purchasing real estate in the San Fernando Valley in the area which became Studio City. Their plan was to build a Movie City, selling the property to studios and production companies and real estate companies (for building housing for the workers at the new studios). Mack Sennett was the first to move to the area from his Edendale location. On 20.1 acres of land (see acreage on next page), he began construction of the Mack Sennett Studio around June 1927. The $800,000 studio was completed in the spring of 1928 and the first filming began there on May 1st. On November 28, 1933, Mack Sennett Inc. was declared bankrupt and he lost the studio. The court-appointed trustee in the case worked for Guaranty Building and Loan. The studio was soon under the ownership of the Guaranty Liquidating Corporation. Mascot Pictures, owned by Nat Levine, in late December 1934, signed a five-year lease for the property to begin January 21, 1935. On October 1, 1935, Mascot sublet the property to Republic Productions Inc.

Republic Pictures was the creation of Herbert J. Yates. He was the owner of the Consolidated Film Industries (CFI), a lab that provided film processing and finances for many companies. In 1935 Yates decided to form his own production company for motion pictures. By using the leverage of past due bills from Monogram Pictures, Mascot Pictures, Liberty Pictures, Majestic Pictures, Chesterfield Pictures, and Invincible Pictures to his CFI, he was able to induce six studios to join with him to form Republic Pictures.

After subleting the Mascot Studio, Republic and Mascot were sued by Guaranty Liquidating Corporation for an illegal transfer of ownership. While the lawsuit was waged in the courts, Republic began to buy up adjoining property to the Mascot lot, including the Christie lot just to the north which housed sets for their films. By the end of November 1936, Republic had obtained ownership on the 15.4 acres adjacent, the 4.8 above that, and the final 2.0 plot (see map next page). On March 14, 1939, the ownership of the original Sennett Studio property was officially under the ownership of Republic.

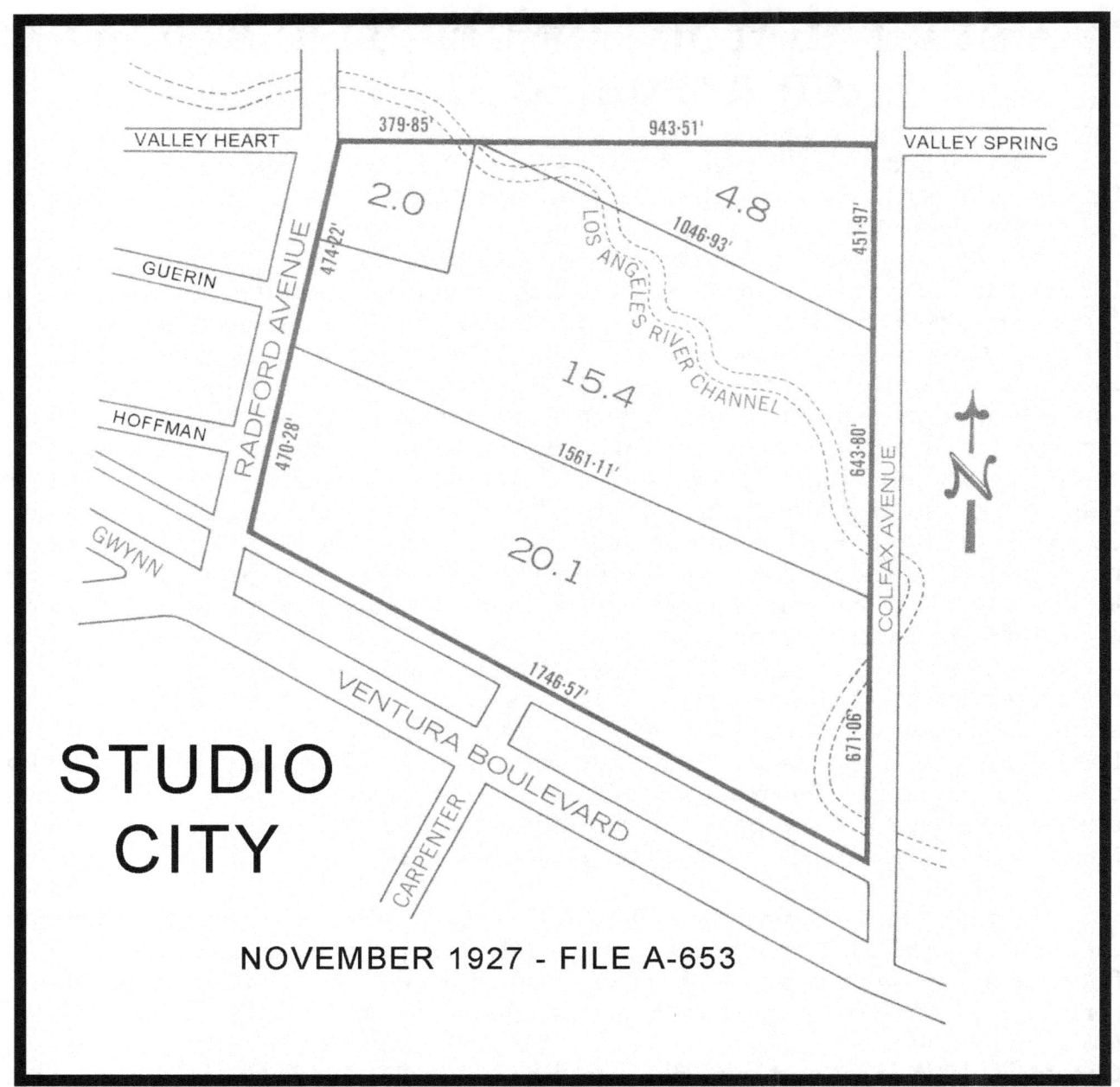

DIRECTIONS TO THE STUDIO: From Los Angeles, take the Hollywood (101) Freeway north. Exit at Ventura Boulevard. Turn left onto Campo de Cahuenga Way. Turn right at Ventura Boulevard. Turn right at Radford Avenue. The studio will be on your right.

A BRIEF LOOK AT THE BACKLOT LOCATIONS

BRAZOS STREET
Built for the 1939 "Man of Conquest" film. These buildings were shells.

DAKOTA STREET
Built in 1945 for John Wayne's "Dakota". A street of false fronts.

DUCHESS RANCH
Built in late 1943, located downslope from Stages 10 and 11. It featured a ranch house shell with three entrances—west, south, and east sides. A barn behind it was also a shell with multiple entrances.

MANSION
Built in 1949 for John Wayne's "The Fighting Kentuckian", this three-sided building (no back or interior) was located behind Stage 10 and between Radford Ave. and the Duchess Ranch. An entrance to the studio and the mansion was located there.

MELODY RANCH
Built in 1940 for Gene Autry's "Melody Ranch" film. The Barn would later become the interior of the My Three Sons house façade.

NEW YORK STREET
Built in 1937 in a T-formation. The main street ran east-west with the south side sporting false fronts and the north were false fronts covering Stages 7 and 13. At the t-intersection, the main set feature was a building that was a theater/opera house and other incarnations. The sets on that side were also false fronts. In a few years, they were the backsie of false fronts on New York Square.

NEW YORK SQUARE
Built in late 1941/early 1942, it was L shaped against rear portions of Western Street and New York Street false-fronts, and faced toward the main lot.

WESTERN STREET
When Trem Carr resigned as president of Republic Productions, Inc., he also did not renew his lease on his movie ranch property where a full scale western town and other sets were located. Those sets were relocated to Ernie Hickson's property at the Placeritos Ranch. Republic now needed to build a western street set on their backlot. Construction began in early 1936. "Winds of the Wasteland" appears to be the first film to use the new sets.

HACIENDA SQUARE
Probably the first set built by Republic Pictures in 1935. There was an entrance gate on the east wall, hacienda building along the north side, another entrance (to the later built Spanish Street) at the northwest corner, and buildings down the left side. There was nothing along the south side. After Western Street was built, to

cover this open area, a variety of buildings and false fronts were utilized to cover the empty area.

SPANISH STREET
Built by 1938. It was a short street.

CANTINA STREET
Built by 1938. Originally known as Mexican Street. It was also a short street heading south from Spanish Street and ending at Western Street.

MEXICAN STREET
Original name for Spanish Street. Later relocated to the north side of Spanish Street.

MINIATURE POOL
Building permit issued February 7, 1944. By January 1, 1938, there was already a small pond there. In 1944, it was cemented in.

UNDERWATER TANK
Built in 1948 for John Wayne's "Wake of the Red Witch". Underwater camera ports photographed action under the water.

* * * * * * * * * *

During the time that Revue Productions leased the studio property for their television shows before purchasing the Universal-International Studio, one of their contracts included a proviso that a Suburban Street was to be constructed. So in 1954, the combination Residential Street (Melody Ranch was converted into two houses), New England Street (which included the first home of the *Leave It To Beaver* television show, and Suburban Street were erected. The fronts of both Suburban Street and New England Street were on the sets of the same buildings, one facing east, the other west.

LAGOON
Built between 1938 and 1941. It would later sport structures along its shores.

CLIFFS AND CAVES
The cliffs and caves set apparently was built in 1940. It featured two separate cliffs with a pathway/roadway between them, and one side featured cave entrances. It was built between the lagoon and Melody Ranch.

CAVE SET (INTERIOR)
Built as part of the original New York Street. It contained interchangeable tunnel segments which could easily be changed depending on script needs. My friend, Steve Lodge, who worked at the studio for several years, stated that it was a tin shed and hot in the summer.

Top: Early photograph showing the location of the studio while still farm land.
Bottom: Early construction on the Mack Sennett Studio.

Above: 1955 aerial photograph of the studio lot looking westward.

Page vi Top: An early view of the main studio lot.
Page vi Bottom: A 1941 aerial view of the backlot.
Page vii Top: A view of the northwest side of the backlot in 1955. Mansion is bottom left, headed in trees, Duchess Ranch is next, the Lagoon is empty of water, the Cliff and Caves set, and the Melody Ranch, already converted into residential housing.
Page vii Bottom: Aerial view of the Miniature Pool and the Underwater Tank

Top: The cave set building, located between the Western Street set and the back side of the Cyclorama.

Middle and Bottom: Two 1956 images of the New York Square. Bottom one includes the Mill Building (curved roof).

ix

Left: The Mansion set.

Middle: Early view of Melody Ranch.

Bottom: A view of the Duchess Ranch.

Top: Dakota Street
Bottom: Brazos Street

THE WESTERN STREET

Above: The new western street (*Winds of the Wasteland*)
Below: A later incarnation of the street with second stories added to the north side

Above: 1941 view of the street (*Bad Men of Deadwood*)
Below: Gene Autry and Smiley Burnette leading a parade

THE MEXICAN, SPANISH, HACIENDA SETS

THE CAVE SET

FORT SET

THE LAGOON AND CLIFFS

NEW ENGLAND STREET

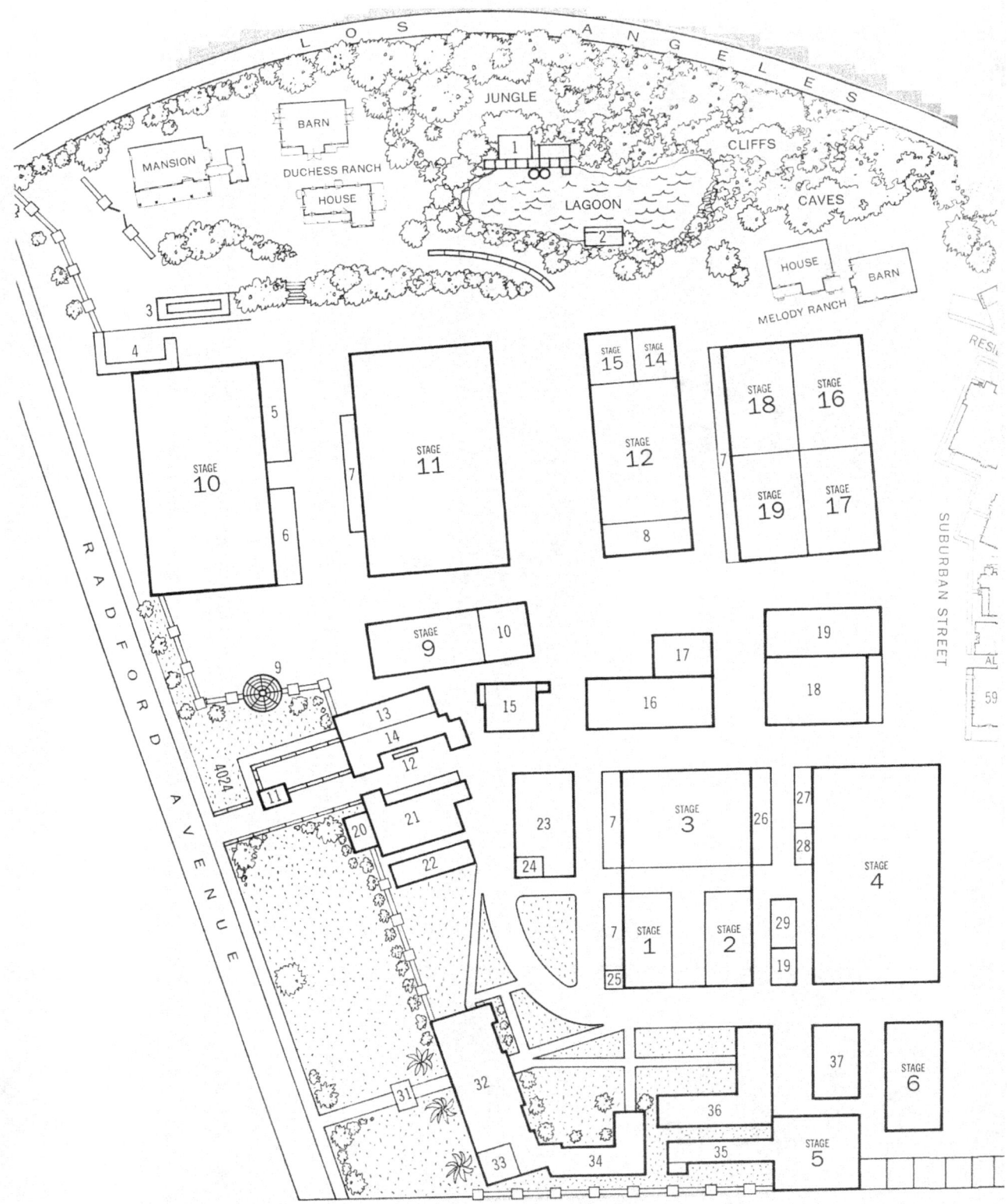

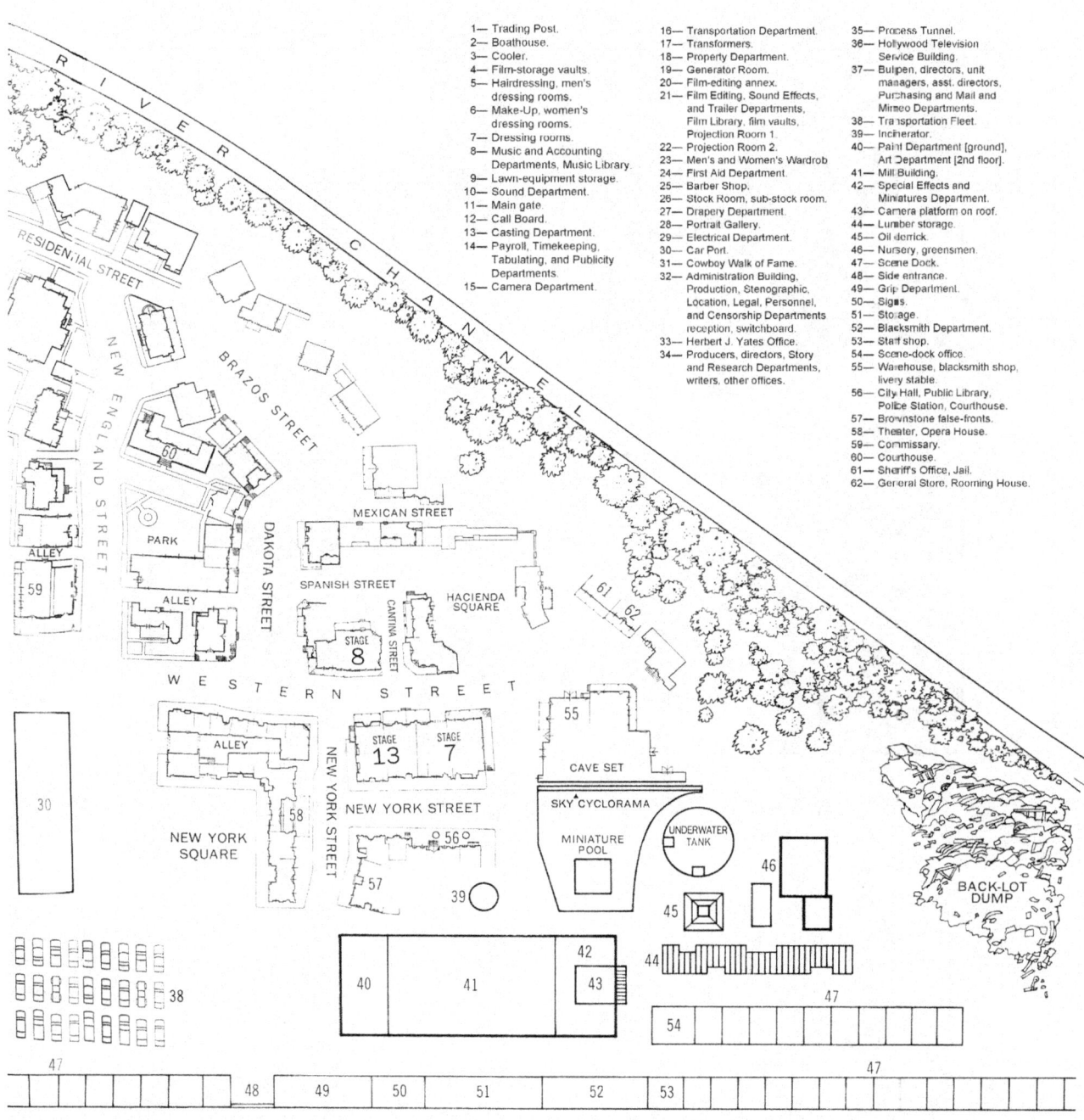

Above: A 1938 aerial photograph of the studio

Above: A 1944 aerial photograph of the studio

Above: A 1952 aerial photograph of the lot

Darkest Africa
(1936)

Directors: B. Reeves Eason and Joseph Kane. **Cast:** Clyde Beatty (Clyde Beatty), Manuel King (Baru Tremaine), Elaine Shepard (Valerie Tremaine), Lucien Prival (Dagna), Bonga (Ray "Crash" Corrigan), Wheeler Oakman (Durkin), Edward McWade (Gorn), Edmund Cobb (Craddock), Ray Turner (Hambone), Donald Reed (Negus).

Synopsis: While on Safari in East Africa, Clyde Beatty runs into a loincloth wearing boy, Baru Tremaine (**Manuel King**), and his pet ape Bonga (**Ray "Crash" Corrigan**). Baru reveals that he has escaped from the lost city of Joba, King Solomon's sacred city of the Golden Bat, but that his sister, Valerie Tremaine (**Elaine Shepard**), remains there. She was found by High Priest Dagna (**Lucien Prival**) as a child and declared to be Joba's goddess as part of his quest for power. Her escape could cause a revolt among the city's citizens. Clyde agrees to help Baru rescue Valerie and they set out to Joba, through the Valley of Lost Souls. Meanwhile, the unscrupulous Durkin (**Wheeler Oakman**) and Craddock (**Edmund Cobb**) notice the green diamond Baru is wearing and follow them to plunder the city for similar jewels. Dagna receives word of the heroes approach from his bat-men and makes plans to stop them.

Locations: Lower Iverson Ranch, Sherwood Forest, Republic Studio backlot and Los Angeles River, King's Jungleland, Brownsville, Texas, and lion cave set.

A flying Batman in the Lower Iverson Ranch in the gorge between the Cliffs of Nyoka and the Garden of the Gods areas (Chapter 1).

Three view of the Lower Iverson Ranch. The Iverson Ranch was a homestead property, at first only the lower portion of the final ranch size was included. Later, the upper portion was added around 1940 by purchasing that homestead from its original owners. From Chapter 2 and two from Chapter 14.

DARKEST AFRICA

The Sherwood Forest area near Lake Sherwood is seen in the top image (Chapter 1).

The lion scenes were filmed at the Brownsville, Texas, facility of the Snake King, William King (born William Abraham Lieberman). His son, Manuel, became a lion tamer at an early age (Chapter 1).

Republic Pictures Studio was located in Studio City, California, at 4024 Radford Avenue.

The Hacienda Square redressed as Africa (Chapter 1).

The native village located on the south banks of the Los Angeles River on studio property (Chapter 1 and 2).

Running through the studio property was the Los Angeles River. Beginning in 1938, the entire length of the river was paved. The studio property portion was still unpaved in 1941 and paved by 1955. Of course, the studio used it as part of their backlot. The first two images are from Chapter 1 and 5, respectively.

Located in a metal building, located behind backlot sets on the western street, were the cave sets. Here is a view of a portion of it from Chapter 3.

Undersea Kingdom
(1936)

Directors: B. Reeves Eason and Joseph Kane. **Cast:** Ray Corrigan (Crash Corrigan), Lois Wilde (Diana Compton), Monte Blue (Unga Khan), William Farnum (Sharad), Boothe Howard (Ditmar), Raymond Hatton (Gasspom), C. Montague Shaw (Norton), Lee Van Atta (Billy Norton), Smiley Burnette (Briny Deep), Frankie Marvin (Salty), Lon Chaney Jr. (Hakur), Lane Chandler (Darius), Jack Mulhall (Andrews), John Bradford (Joe), Malcolm McGregor (Zogg), Ralph Holmes (Martos), John Merton (Moloch), Ernie Smith (Gourck), Lloyd Whitlock (Clinton).

Synopsis: Lieutenant Crash Corrigan (**Ray "Crash" Corrigan**), in his last year at the United States Naval Academy in Annapolis, Maryland, is invited by Billy Norton (**Lee Van Atta**) to visit his father, Professor Norton (**C. Montague Shaw**), after a wrestling match. At their house, the professor is demonstrating his new invention, which can detect and prevent (at short range) earthquakes, to Diana Compton (**Lois Wilde**) and his theory about regular tremours from the area where Atlantis used to be. When Atlantean tyrant Unga Khan (**Monte Blue**) and his Black Robe army turn their Disintegrator beam on St. Clair, Professor Norton leads an expedition to investigate. Along with him in his Rocket Submarine are Crash, Diana, three sailors, Briny Deep (**Smiley Burnette**), Salty (**Frankie Marvin**), and Joe (**John Bradford**) and their pet parrot Sinbad. Unknown to the expedition until it is underway and in trouble, Billy has stowed away on the Rocket Sub as well.

Locations: Lower Iverson Ranch, Republic Studio front lot, backlot, and Los Angeles River.

Stock Footage of Annapolis (Chapter 1).

UNDERSEA KINGDOM

Three views of the Lower Iverson Ranch (Chapter 4, 2 and 1, respectively).

The Devil's Doorway (Chapter 2) was a rock formation which could be easily traversed by foot or on horseback. It was one of three different locations with a similar feature on the ranch.

An early view of the interior and exterior of the cave set on the backlot of Republic Studios (Chapter 1 and 2).

Unknown building on the front lot (possibly Camera Department) (Chapter 1).

UNDERSEA KINGDOM

The Los Angeles River Bed which divided the main portion of the studio from the northern portion (Chapter 2).

The Hacienda Square (Chapter 4).

The Hacienda Square with a matte painting (Chapter 1).

UNDERSEA KINGDOM

The three images on this page are from Chapter 1 and have not been identified as to location at this time. They were filmed by a second unit with stand-ins/body doubles for the shots.

The Vigilantes Are Coming (1936)

Directors: Mack V. Wright and Ray Taylor. **Cast:** Robert Livingston (Don Loring), Kay Hughes (Doris Colton), Guinn (Big Boy) Williams (Salvation), Raymond Hatton (Whipsaw), Fred Kohler (Jason Burr), Robert Warwick (Ivan Raspinoff), William Farnum (Father Jose), Bob Kortman (Boris Petroff), John Merton (Rance Talbot), Lloyd Ingraham (John Colton), William Dismond (Anderson), Yakima Canutt (Barsam), Tracy Layne (Clem Peters), Bub Pope (Ivan), Steve Clemente (Pedro), Bud Osborne (Harris).

Synopsis: Following the discovery of gold in Mexican California in 1844, Russian Cossacks led by Count Ivan Raspinoff (**Robert Warwick**), in collusion with General Jason Burr (**Fred Kohler**), attempt to invade California and turn it into a Russian Colony with Burr as its dictator. In doing so they round up slaves to work the mines and General Burr has Don Loring's brother and father murdered to acquire their ore-rich land. When Don (**Robert Livingston**) returns, having been away at the time with Salvation (**Guinn "Big Boy" Williams**), Whipsaw (**Raymond Hatton**), and Captain John Fremont (**Ray "Crash" Corrigan**), he assumes the masked identity of The Eagle to stop them and get his revenge. He is aided by a group of vigilantes assembled from the Californian ranchers, fighting both General Burr's henchmen and Raspinoff's Cossacks, while awaiting the arrival of Captain Fremont's American troops before the colony becomes official.

Locations: Kernville, San Fernando Mission, Mission San Luis Rey, Pala Mission, Republic Studio backlot.

The Pala Mission ruins located at 11798 Pala Mission Rd, Pala, California (Chapter 1).

Two views of the Mission San Luis Rey, in Oceanside, California (Chapter 1).

The Pala Mission (Chapter 3).

THE VIGILANTES ARE COMING

The San Fernando Mission (Chapter 1).

The Hacienda Square on the backlot of Republic Studios (Chapter 8).

Kernville, California (Chapter 1).

Kernville River (Chapter 2).

Kernville (Chapter 2).

The original town of Kernville and most of the area surrounding it are now at the bottom of Lake Isabella. A dam was erected a few years after this serial was filmed there, which flooded the entire valley.

THE VIGILANTES ARE COMING

Kernville (Chapter 3).

Kernville (Chapter 5).

Kernville (Chapter 5).

Robinson Crusoe of Clipper Island (1936)

Directors: Mack V. Wright and Ray Taylor. **Cast:** Mala (Mala), Mamo Clark (Melani), Herbert Rawlinson (Grant Jackson), William Newell (Hank McGlaurie), John Ward (Anthony Tupper), John Dilson (E. G. Ellsworth), Selmer Jackson (Canfield), John Piccori (Porotu), George Chesebro (Draker), Robert Kortman (Wilson), George Cleveland (Goebel), Lloyd Whitlock (Lamar), Tiny Roebuck (Eppa), Tracy Layne (Larkin), Herbert Weber (Stevens), Anthony Pawley (Clark), Allen Connor (Jim Taylor).

Synopsis: Agent Mala (**Ray Mala**), an intelligence operative, investigates sabotage on the remote *Clipper Island*. A gang of spies causes the eruption of a volcano, for which Mala is blamed. He convinces the native Princess Melani (**Mamo Clark**) of his innocence and helps her ward off a takeover by rival high priest and spy collaborator Porotu (**John Piccori**) and discover the identity of spy ringleader *H.K.* (**Selmer Jackson**).

Locations: Bronson Canyon, Santa Cruz Island and Valdez Cove Caves, Republic Studio backlot.

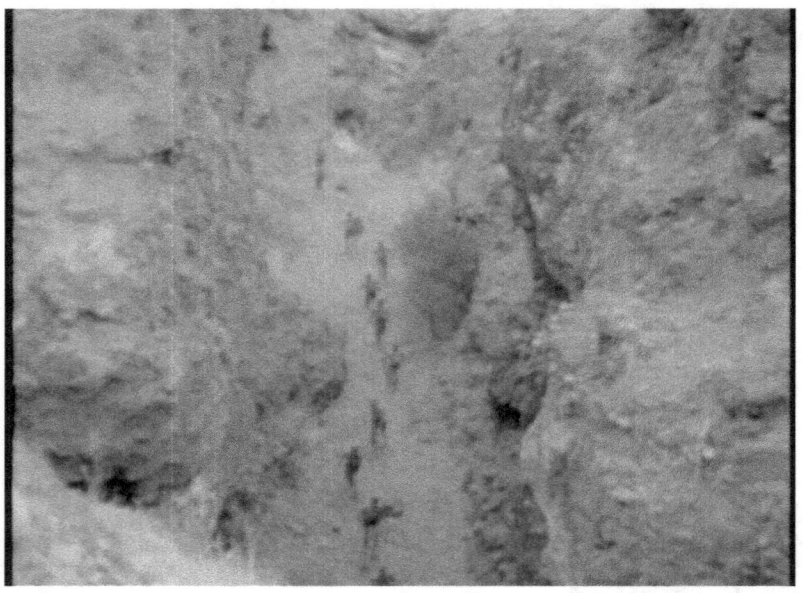

Unidentified location (Chapter 2).

Two views of the Republic Studios backlot on the northern side of the main lot next to the Los Angeles River (Chapter 2).

The Underwater Tank on the Republic Studio backlot (Chapter 3).

Santa Cruz Island off the coast of Southern California (Chapter 2).

Santa Cruz Island (Chapter 2).

Santa Cruz Island (Chapter 4).

Santa Cruz Island, Valdez Cove Caves (Chapter 2).

Santa Cruz Island, Valdez Cove Caves (Chapter 4).

Santa Cruz Island, Valdez Cove Caves (Chapter 2).

Two views of Bronson Canyon (Chapter 4).

Dick Tracy
(1937)

Directors: Ray Taylor and Alan James. **Cast:** Ralph Byrd (Dick Tracy), Kay Hughes (Gwen Andrews), Smiley Burnette (Mike McGurk), Lee Van Atta (Junior), John Piccori (Moloch), Carleton Young (Gordon Tracy (after)), Fred Hamilton (Steve Lockwood), Francis X. Bushman (Clive Anderson), John Dilson (Ellery Brewster), Richard Beach (Gordon Tracy (before)), Wedgewood Nowell (H. T. Clayton), Theodore Lorch (Patorno), Edwin Stanley (Walter Odette), Harrison Greene (Cloggerstein), Herbert Weber (Tony Marino), Buddy Roosevelt (Burke), George DeNormand (Flynn), Byron K. Foulger (Korvitch), Oscar and Elmer.

Synopsis: Dick Tracy's (**Ralph Byrd**) foe for this serial is the crime boss and masked mystery villain the Spider/the Lame One (both names are used) and his Spider Ring. In the process of various crimes, including using his flying wing and sound weapon to destroy the Bay Bridge in San Francisco and stealing an experimental "speed plane", The Spider captures Dick Tracy's brother, Gordon Tracy (**Richard Beach**). The Spider's minion, Dr. Moloch (**John Piccori**), performs a brain operation on Gordon Tracy (**Carleton Young**) to turn him evil, making him secretly part of the Spider Ring and so turning brother against brother.

Locations: Redondo Steam Plant, Van Nuys City Hall, Van Nuys, Union Air Terminal, Burbank, Pacific Light and Power Co., Redondo Beach, California Stucco Co., Coldwater Canyon/Mulholland Drive; East 4th Street near 4th Place, Souther Pacific Central Station, East 4th Place and Mateo Street, Santa Fe Ave. under East 4th Place, second unit for Alcatraz, San Francisco F.BI field office, San Francisco City Hall, San Francisco Bay and Pier 22, and San Francisco Bay Bridge.

Second Unit of the San Francisco F.B.I. field office (Chapter 1).

A vintage view of the Union Air Terminal in Burbank, California (later renamed Bob Hope Airport).

The Union Air Terminal (Chapter 2).

Louie's Coffee Shop, 14445 Sylvan Street, Van Nuys (Chapter 14).

Van Nuys City Hall and Police Station, 14410 Sylvan Street (Chapter 14).

The corner of Sylmar Ave. and Sylvan Street, Van Nuys (probably the southeast corner) (Chapter 14).

The Pacific Light and Power Comapny Steam Plant in Redondo Beach (Chapter 15). The plant was demolished in 1946 and replaced with a newer plant.

Santa Fe Ave. under East 4th Place, near downtown Los Angeles (Chapter 1).

East 4th Place and Mateo Street, near downtown Los Angeles (Chapter 1).

East 4th Street near East 4th Place, near downtown Los Angeles (Chapter 1).

Coldwater Canyon and Mulholland Drive, Los Angeles (Chapter 1).

California Stucco Co., 1803 East 25th Street, Los Angeles (Chapter 1).

Southern Pacific Central Station at Central Avenue and 5th Street (Chapter 1). Probably stock shot.

Republic Studios backlot (Chapter 7).

Republic Studios backlot cave set (Chapter 7).

Republic Studios backlot New York Street (Chapter 1).

Republic Studios front lot (Chapter 1).

San Francisco Bay, Pier 22 (Chapter 3).

The Painted Stallion (1937)

Directors: William Witney, Alan James, and Ray Taylor. **Cast:** Ray Corrigan (Clark Stuart), Hoot Gibson (Walter Jamison), LeRoy Mason (Alfredo Dupray), Duncan Renaldo (Zamorro), Sammy McKim (Kit Carson), Hal Taliaferro (Jim Bowie), Jack Perrin (Davy Crockett), Oscar and Elmer (Oscar and Elmer), Julia Thayer (The Rider), Yakima Canutt (Tom), Matson Williams (Macklin), Duke Taylor (Bill), Loren Riebe (Pedro), George DeNormand (Oldham), Gordon DeMain (Governor), Charles King (Bull Smith), Vinegar Roan (Pete).

Synopsis: A wagon train travelling from Independence, Missouri to Santa Fe means trouble for Alfredo Dupray (**LeRoy Mason**), his authority from Spain will end with the arrival of a Mexican Governor. He plots to solve this by intercepting a trade agreement, to be negotiated by Clark Stuart (**Ray "Crash" Corrigan**) on the wagon train, and disrupt Mexico–United States relations. Repeated attacks are thwarted, however, by the appearance of a mysterious Rider (**Julia Thayer**) on a Painted Stallion who issues warnings with her whistling arrows. With her help Clark Stuart, along with historical characters, Kit Carson (**Sammy McKim**), Jim Bowie (**Hal Taliaferro**), and Davy Crockett (**Jack Perrin**) work to defeat Dupray.

Locations: Lasky Mesa, Bronson Canyon Caves, Lake Sherwood, Republic Studio backlot, and Snow Canyon in Utah.

Stock footage from Tim McCoy's silent film, *War Paint* (Chapter 1).

THE PAINTED STALLION

Three views of Snow Canyon area, west of St. George, Utah.

Chapter 1.

Chapter 1.

Chapter 2.

Lasky Mesa/Ahmanson Ranch/Upper Las Virgenes Open Space, located northwest of Calabasas and Woodland Hills (Chapter 7).

Lasky Mesa (Chapter 7).

Lasky Mesa (Chapter 7).

Republic Studios backlot Hacienda Square (Chapter 1).

Republic Studios backlot Western Street (Chapter 1).

Republic Studios backlot Cave Set (Chapter 4).

Three views of Bronson Canyon.

Chapter 12.

Chapter 11.

Chapter 3.

Kernville (Chapter 3).

Lake Sherwood (Chapter 4)

S. O. S. Coast Guard
(1937)

Directors: William Witney and Alan James. **Cast:** Ralph Byrd (Terry Kent), Bela Lugosi (Boroff), Maxine Doyle (Jean Norman), Richard Alexander (Thorg), Lee Ford (Snapper McGree), Herbert Rawlinson (Boyle), John Picorri (G. A. Rackerby), Lawrence Grant (Rabinisi), Thomas Carr (Jim Kent), Carleton Young (Dodds), Allen Connor (Dick Norman), George Chesebro (L. H. DeGado), Ranny Weeks (Wells).

Synopsis: Boroff (**Bela Lugosi**) is a mad scientist who has invented a "disintegrator gas" and plans to smuggle it to his buyers in Morovania. When his ship, the *Carfax*, gets stranded on outlying rocks in the first chapter, the Coast Guard comes to rescue him. Recognized by the reporters, Jean Norman (**Maxine Doyle**) and Snapper McGree (**Lee Ford**), Boroff runs and kills the pursuing Coast Guard Ensign Jim Kent (**Thomas Carr**), who turns out to be Lt. Terry Kent's brother (**Ralph Byrd**).

Locations: Hollywood Riviera Beach Club, Stearns Wharf, Bluff Cove, White Point Hot Springs, Santa Monica Pier, Potassium Phosphate Inc., Santa Suana Depot, Hueneme, El Miro Theater, 240 Broadway in Santa Monica, and Republic Studio backlot.

Hollywood Riviera Beach Club, Torrance. Burned down in 1958. Location is now a park along Paseo de la Playa (Chapter 1).

Santa Monica Pier (Chapter 3).

Chatsworth Depot (Chapter 6).

Stock shot from *Robinson Crusoe on Clipper Island* (Chapter 1).

Bronson Canyon (Chapter 12).

Main Street Bridge, Santa Monica. Approximate location is Triangle Square at Colorado Avenue and Main Street (Chapter 10).

El Miro Theater, 1441 3rd Street, Santa Monica (Chapter 10).

Truck is passing 240 Broadway, Santa Monica (Chapter 10).

Location is probably the corner of 4th and Idaho, Santa Monica (Chapter 10).

Republic Studios backlot New York Street (Chapter 2).

Three views of Bluff Cove, located just south of Palos Verdes.

Chapter 11.

Chapter 3.

Chapter 3.

White Point Hot Springs, Palos Verdes. Built at the location of a Japanese fishing village, two brothers, Tojuro and Tamiji Tagami, in 1910 discovered a sulfur hot springs at the site. They built a two-story hotel and restaurant, a bathhouse, and a swimming pool filled with ocean water. By the late 1930s, the resort was closed to damage to the structures from storms and earthquakes.

All three images are from Chapter 4.

The Potassium Phosphate Inc. was located at 2810 S. Pacific Ave., San Pedro, on land just south of Fort MacArthur. Its former site is now inside of the current fort's perimeter and all of its buildings are long gone.

All three images are from Chapter 4.

Above: An aerial view of Fort MacArthur with the Potassium Phosphate plant (aka Trona) is on the far right.

Below: An aerial view of Fort MacArthur with the Potassium Phosphate plant (Trona) in the upper left portion of the image.

Three views of scenes shot at Stearns Wharf, Santa Barbara.

Chapter 3.

Chapter 2.

Chapter 2.

Three views of the Hueneme Wharf prior to its destruction with the building of Port Hueneme.

Chapter 8.

Chapter 9.

Chapter 9.

Zorro Rides Again
(1937)

Directors: William Witney and John English. **Cast:** Zorro, Helen Christian (Joyce Andrews), Reed Howes (Philip Andrews), Duncan Renaldo (Renaldo), Noah Beery (J. A. Marsden), Richard Alexander (Brad Dace), John Carroll (James Vega), Nigel de Brulier (Don Manual Vega), Robert Kortman (Trelliger), Jack Ingram (Carter), Roger Williams (Manning), Edmund Cobb (Larkin), Mona Rico (Carmelita), Tom London (O'Shea), Harry Strang (O'Brien), Jerry Frank (Duncan).

Synopsis: In contemporary California, villain J. A. Marsden (**Noah Beery Sr.**) aims to take over the California-Yucatan Railroad with the aid of his henchman Brad "El Lobo" Dace (**Richard Alexander**). The rightful owners, Joyce (**Helen Christian**) and Phillip Andrews (**Reed Howes**), naturally object. Their partner, Don Manuel Vega (**Nigel De Brulier**) summons his nephew, James Vega (**John Carroll**), to help them as he is the great grandson of the original Zorro, Don Diego de la Vega. He is disappointed, however, to find that his nephew is a useless fop. Nevertheless, James Vega installs himself in the original Zorro's hideout and adopts the Zorro identity to defeat Marsden and El Lobo. This Zorro uses twin pistols and a whip as his main weapons of choice, rather than a more traditional sword.

Locations: Lower Iverson Ranch, Bronson Canyon, Red Rock Canyon, Chatsworth Train Cut and Tunnel, Pacoima Dam, Southern Pacific Railroad/San Fernando Pass, Republic Studio backlot, Trem Carr Ranch stock footage, Kernville stock footage, Lone Pine stock footage.

Located just south of the Iverson Movie Ranch, the train tracks, after leaving the first tunnel, head through a cut in the mountain towards a second tunnel. This is a stock shock used many times by a variety of films from Republic Pictures (Chapter 3).

The first Chatsworth Train Tunnel—Santa Susana Pass Road ran over the top and to the north side, close to the Iverson Movie Ranch (Chapter 9).

Palmdale area (Chapter 1).

Republic Studios backlot cave set (Chapter 1).

Red Rock Canyon, located in Cantil. Filming took place in Hagen Canyon, just south of Abbott Road.

Chapter 1.

Chapter 1.

Chapter 3.

Three views of the Southern Pacific Railroad tracks in the San Fernando Pass area, south of Sierra Highway. All from Chapter 3.

Three views of the Pacoima Reservoir and Dam is located at the northern end of Pacoima Canyon Road just north of Sylmar. All images on this page are from Chapter 8

ZORRO RIDES AGAIN

Above: Filming a scene from the serial atop the Pacoima Dam.
Below: The approach to the dam during the filming days (Chapter 9).

The Lower Iverson Ranch.

The Garden of the Gods (Chapter 1).

Zorro rearing his horse at the future "Lone Ranger Rock" from the television series of the 1950's (Chapter 4).

Heading down into the gorge. A glimpse of the Nyoka Cliff is on the left, and a portion of the Santa Susana Mountains in the background (Chapter 4).

The Lower Iverson Ranch.

The Nyoka Cliff is the main feature in this image (Chapter 4).

Chapter 9.

Chapter 12.

Three views of the Republic Studio backlot.

Store fronts for a city view (Chapter 3).

Closeup of a store front (Chapter 3).

An early set on the backlot (Chapter 3).

ZORRO RIDES AGAIN

Three views of the Republic Studio backlot.

An early view of the Western Street (Chapter 2).

Western Street archway to Cantina Street Chapter 2).

Hacienda Square building (Chapter 4).

The Fillmore to Valencia railroad line many times by Republic Pictures, including as stock footage.

Chapter 3.

The Bronson Canyon Caves area (Chapter 1).

The road leading to the Bronson Canyon Caves. It is still there and is still unpaved (Chapter 1).

The Lone Ranger (1938)

Directors: William Witney and John English. **Cast:** The Lone Ranger (Lee Powell), Silver Chief (Silver), Lynn Roberts (Joan Blanchard), Stanley Andrews (Mark Smith), George Cleveland (George Blanchard), William Farnum (Father McKim), Chief Thunder-Cloud (Tonto), Hal Taliaferro (Bob Stuart), Herman Brix (Bert Rogers), Lee Powell (Allen King), Lane Chandler (Dick Forrest), George Letz (Jim Clark), John Merton (Kester), Sammy McKim (Sammy), Tom London (Felton), Raphael Bennet (Black Taggart), Maston Williams (Joe Snead), Frank McGlynn Sr (Abraham Lincoln).

Synopsis: In 1865, Captain Mark Smith (**Stanley Andrews**) of the Confederate Army leads a band of deserters to conquer Texas and rule it as a dictator. In one of his first actions, he captures and assumes the identity of Texas's new Finance Commissioner, Colonel Marcus Jeffries, after having the real man murdered. When a contingent of Texas Rangers enters the territory, Joe Snead (**Maston Williams**), one of Smith's men, leads them into an ambush by Smith's "troopers". The Rangers are apparently wiped out, although one injured survivor is left. The survivor, nursed back to health by Tonto (**Chief Thundercloud**), swears to avenge the massacre and defeat "Colonel Jeffries" and his men. When he is not operating as the Ranger, he appears under an assumed identity as one of a group of Texans resisting Smith's rule. Smith, through a henchman, has narrowed the field of suspects down to five specific members of the resistance. One of these five—Allen King (**Lee Powell**), Bob Stuart (**Hal Taliaferro**), Bert Rogers (**Herman Brix**), Dick Forrest (**Lane Chandler**), and Jim Clark (**George Letz**)—actually is the Ranger, but only Tonto and the other four Texans know which one it is. Together, they operate as an effective team attempting to end Smith's rule.

Locations: Lower Iverson Ranch, Lone Pine, Republic Studio backlot.

The Owens River Valley near Lone Pine.

THE LONE RANGER

Three views of Lone Pine. All images for this serial were supplied from the feature film version of the serial: *Hi-Yo Silver*. The only film prints available for the serial are in very bad shape.

The ambush scene where Tonto finds the Lone Ranger.

THE LONE RANGER

The Lower Iverson Ranch.

The Aaron Iverson barn.

Looking away from the above barn towards the Garden of the Gods and beyond.

Republic Pictures Studio backlot.

Entrance to Hacienda Square.

Cantina Street.

Spanish Street.

THE LONE RANGER

Republic Studio backlot.

The upper portion of the western most building on the north side of Spanish Street.

Hacienda Square.

Western Street.

The Fighting Devil Dogs (1938)

Directors: William Witney and John English. **Cast:** Lee Powell (Tom Grayson), Herman Brix (Frank Corby), Eleanor Stewart (Janet Warfield), Montagu Love (White), Hugh Sothern (Ben Warfield), Sam Flint (Grayson), Perry Ivins (Crenshaw), Forrest Taylor (Benson), John Picorri (Gould), Carleton Young (Johnson), John Davidson (Lin Wing), Henry Otho (Sam Hedges), Reed Howes (Parker), Tom London (Wilson), Edmund Cobb (Ellis), Alan Gregg (Macro), Allan Mathews (Todd).

Synopsis: In Singapore, two Marine Lieutenants, Tom Grayson (**Lee Powell**) and Frank Corby (**Herman Brix**), uncover the threat of a masked terrorist called the Lightning, who uses an arsenal of powerful lightning-based weaponry in his bid for world conquest. However, the battle becomes personal when the Lightning annihilates the officers' unit and later kills Lt. Grayson's father (**Sam Flint**) as he was helping the investigation of the weapon. Now, the marines have dedicated themselves to stopping the Lightning and bringing him to justice.

Locations: Lake Sherwood, Beale's Cut, Republic Studio backlot and L.A. River.

The Alley on the south side of Republic Studio heading towards Radford Avenue (Chapter 3).

THE FIGHTING DEVIL DOGS

Lake Sherwood (Chapter 1).

Sherwood Forest area (Chapter 2).

Sherwood Forest area (Chapter 2).

Descanso Beach, Catalina Island (Chapter 5).

Republic Studio backlot cave set (Chapter 4).

A portion of the Los Angeles River which cut through the Republic Studio property (Chapter 6).

THE FIGHTING DEVIL DOGS

Republic Studio backlot.

New York Street (Chapter 3).

New York Street (Chapter 1).

Republic Studio front lot buildings (Chapter 2).

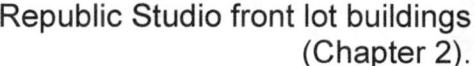

Dick Tracy Returns
(1938)

Directors: William Witney and John English. **Cast:** Ralph Byrd (Dick Tracy), Lynn Roberts (Gwen Andrews), Charles Middleton (Pa Stark), Jerry Tucker (Junior), David Sharpe (Ron Merton), Lee Ford (Mike McGurk), Michael Kent (Steve Lockwood), John Merton (Champ Stark), Raphael Bennett (Trigger Stark), Jack Roberts (Dude Stark), Ned Glass (Kid Stark), Edward Foster (Joe Hanner), Alan Gregg (Jimmy Madison), Reed Howes (Rance), Robert Terry (Reynolds), Tom Seidel (Hunt), Jack Ingram (Slasher Stark).

Synopsis: Dick Tracy (**Ralph Byrd**) and his group must battle saboteurs and spies in his effort to bring down the Stark gang, a major crime family syndicate led by the vicious and brutal Pa Stark (**Charles Middleton**). A young promising G-Man named Ron Merton (**David Sharpe**) is murdered by the Starks while trying to help Tracy bring the gang to justice. With the help of his friends Gwen Andrews (**Lynne Roberts**), Junior (**Jerry Tucker**), and Mike McGurk (**Lee Ford**), Tracy battles the vile criminal gang.

Locations: Bronson Canyon, Pilgrimage Theater, City of Burbank, 761 S. Normandie Ave., Chatsworth Depot, Potassium Phosphate Inc., Van Nuys City Hall, Republic Studio backlot.

Tom's Hardware was located at 229 N. San Fernando Blvd. in Burbank (Chapter 1).

Hotel Darms, 233 N. San Fernando Blvd, Burbank (Chapter 1).

150 N. San Fernando Blvd, Burbank (Chapter 1).

Verdugo Sign Shop, 221 N. Orange Grove Ave, Burbank (Chapter 1). As the truck swings around the corner and heads down Orange Grove Ave., it will pass several homes and businesses, including the Verdugo Sign Shop.

The Potassium Phosphate Inc., 2810 S. Pacific Ave., San Pedro.

Chapter 5.

Chapter 7.

Chapter 7.

Terminal Island Federal Prison on Reservation Point was opened in 1938 and continues to this day as a working prison for male immates. All three images on this page are from Chapter 12.

The Eighth & Normandie Garage, 761 S. Normandie Ave. (Chapter 2).

An interior shot (Chapter 2).

The business is no longer a garage. After an ownership change, it was converted into a storage locker business.

Looking up at the outside of the building (Chapter 2).

The Pilgrimage Theatre was built in 1920. Now known as the John Anson Ford Amphitheater, it is located at 2580 Cahuenga Blvd E, above Hollywood.

All three images are from Chapter 4.

The Bronson Canyon Caves.

Chapter 6.

Chapter 6.

The interior of the main shaft (Chapter 4).

Republic Studio backlot.

New York Street (Chapter 1).

New York Street (Chapter 14).

Chapter 10.

Stock Shots:

Iverson Ranch (Chapter 3).

Griffith Park Observatory (Chapter 4).

F.B.I. San Francisco Field Office (Chapter 1).

The old Van Nuys City Hall and Police Station, 14410 Sylvan Street, Van Nuys.

West Side of the building (Chapter 11).

West Side entrance, now no longer accessible, (Chapter 11).

Exiting the East Side (Chapter 11).

Republic Studio Front Lot.

All three images are from a sequence in Chapter 14.

Hawk of the Wilderness (1938)

Directors: William Witney and John English. **Cast:** Herman Brix (Kioga), Mala (Kias), Monte Blue (Yellow Weasel), Jill Martin (Beth Munro), Noble Johnson (Mokuyi), William Royle (Manuel Solerno), Tom Chatterton (Edward Munro), George Eldredge (Allan Kendle), Patrick J. Kelly (William Williams), Dick Wessel (Dirk), Snowflake (George), Tuffy (Tawnee).

Synopsis: Dr. Lincoln Rand (**Lane Chandler**), leading an expedition to an uncharted island in the Arctic Circle that he theorizes may be the ancestral home of all Native Americans, is shipwrecked. The only survivors are Lincoln Rand Jr. (**Herman Brix**) (Dr Rand's infant son) and the doctor's servant Mokuyi (**Noble Johnson**). Years later, a message in a bottle from the sinking ship is found, and a second expedition led by a Dr. Munro (**Tom Chatterton**) sets out to find the lost expedition. Part of the crew, led by a smuggler named Manuel Solerno (**William Royle**), mutinies when they reach the island, abandoning the doctor's expedition. Dr. Munro and company are rescued by Lincoln Rand Jr, now an adult Tarzan-like character known by the name "Kioga, Hawk of the Wilderness", who was raised to manhood on the island by Mokuyi.

Locations: Iverson Ranch, Bronson Canyon, Lake Sherwood, Mammoth Lakes, probably Abalone Cove, Republic Studio backlot.

Republic Studios backlot cave set (Chapter 1).

Three views of the Mammoth Lakes area.

Chapter 1.

Chapter 1.

Chapter 2.

Three views of Mammoth Lakes from Chapter 5.

Sherwood Lake (all images this page from Chapter 1).

The Bronson Canyon Caves (all three images are from Chapter 11).

Lower Iverson Movie Ranch.

Chapter 12.

Chapter 12.

Chapter 1.

HAWK OF THE WILDERNESS

This location is most likely the Abalone Cove, Palos Verdes.

Chapter 4.

Chapter 1.

Chapter 1.

Republic Studio backlot. The native village, of which there were two separate ones on either side of the Los Angeles River, was probably the one located on the north side of the river (Chapter 2).

The Miniature Pool (Chapter 4).

The backlot Los Angeles River (Chapter 4).

The Lone Ranger Rides Again
(1939)

Directors: William Witney and John English. **Cast:** Robert Livingston (The Lone Ranger), Chief Thunder Cloud (Tonto), Silver Chief (Silver), Duncan Renaldo (Juan Vasquez), Jinx Falken (Sue Dolan), Ralph Dunn (Bart Dolan), J. Farrell MacDonald (Craig Dolan), William Gould (Jed Scott), Rex Lease (Evans), Ted Mapes (Merritt), Henry Otho (Pa Daniels), John Beach (Hardin), Glenn Strange (Thorne), Stanley Blystone (Murdock), Edwin Parker (Hank), Al Taylor (Colt), Carlton Young (Logan).

Synopsis: Homesteaders moving into a valley in New Mexico are being attacked by the Black Raiders. The valley had been settled by rancher Craig Dolan (**J. Farrell MacDonald**), who does not want the new homesteaders to be there. His son, Bart (**Ralph Dunn**), has taken matters into his own hands and formed the Black Raiders. The Lone Ranger (**Robert Livingston**) attempts to aid the homesteaders but he is hampered by his having been framed for being part of the Raiders. In particular, Juan Vasquez (**Duncan Renaldo**) believes that he killed his brother, although when this is disproven he becomes another of the Lone Ranger's partners. However, the Ranger is forced to remove the mask and operate under the name of "Bill Andrews" at times in order to successfully protect the homesteaders.

Locations: Iverson Movie Ranch, Corriganville, Red Rock Canyon, Bronson Canyon, Kernville, Narrows at Towsley Canyon (stock footage), and Republic Studio backlot.

Republic Studios backlot cave set (Chapter 2).

Three views of the Kernville area.

Chapter 3.

Chapter 1.

Chapter 1.

THE LONE RANGER RIDES AGAIN

Three views of Vasquez Rocks.

Chapter 5.

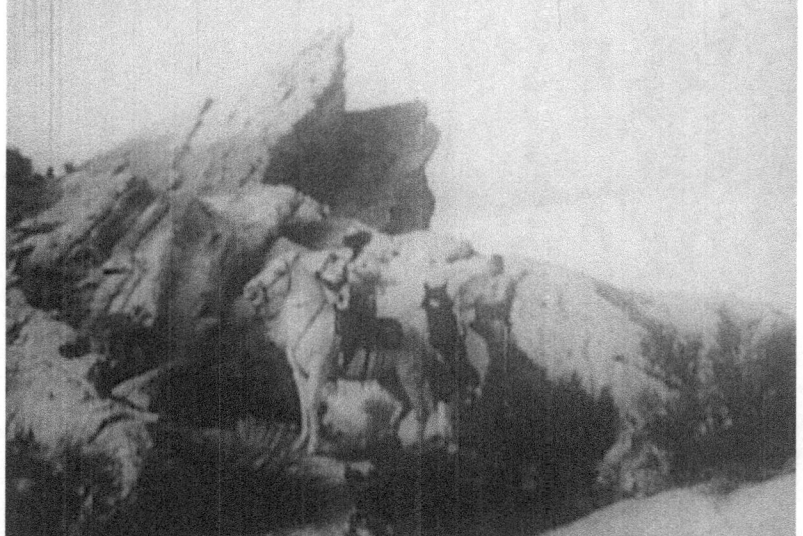

Chapter 1.

Chapter 5.

Red Rock Canyon's Hagen Canyon is shown in these three images.

Chapter 9.

Chapter 1.

Chapter 15.

Three views of the newly opened Corriganville Movie Ranch, owned by Ray "Crash" Corrigan, and located in the eastern end of Simi Valley (all from Chapter 14).

Lower Iverson Movie Ranch.

Chapter 1.

Chapter 1.

Chapter 1. This set was built by 20th Century Fox for the Shirley Temple film *Wee Willie Winkie*.

Lower Iverson Movie Ranch.

Chapter 1.

Chapter 3.

Garden of the Gods, Chapter 4.

Republic Studio backlot.

Early version of the Western Street (Chapter 3).

A fuller view of the Western Street (Chapter 9).

The backlot Cave Set (Chapter 4).

Daredevils of the Red Circle (1939)

Directors: William Witney and John English. **Cast:** Charles Quigley (Gene Townley), Herman Brix (Tiny Dawson), David Sharpe (Burt Knowles), Carole Landis (Blanche Granville), Miles Mander (Horace Granville), Charles Middleton (Harry Crowell/39013), C. Montague Shaw (Malcolm), Ben Taggart (Dixon), William Pagan (Landon), Corbet Morris (Klein), Raymond Bailey (Stanley), Snowflake (Snowflake), George Chesebro (Sheffield), Ray Miller (Jeff), Robert Winkler (Sammy Townley), Tuffie (Tuffie).

Synopsis: The Daredevils of the Red Circle are three college athletes Gene Townley (**Charles Quigley**), Tiny Dawson (**Herman Brix**), and Bert Knowles (**David Sharpe**), who are employed at an amusement enterprise which number 39013 (**Charles Middleton**) destroys. The younger brother of one of the athletes is killed during the havoc and the trio pledge themselves to track down the man responsible.

Locations: George Lewis Estate (stock footage), Ocean Blvd. and McClure Tunnel in Santa Monica, Sea Cliff, Los Angeles Gas and Electric, Giambastian Fuel & Supply Co., Forest Lawn Drive, and Republic Studio backlot.

McClure Tunnel as it heads under Ocean Avenue, Santa Monica (Chapter 1).

Three views of the Sea Cliff area. All images are from Chapter 2.

The Los Angeles Gas & Electric Co., 549 Aliso Street, Los Angeles.

Chapter 2.

Chapter 2.

Across the street from L.A. Gas & Electric was the Giambastian Fuel & Supply Co, 712 Keller Street (Chapter 2).

The Los Angeles Gas & Electric Co., 549 Aliso Street, Los Angeles.

Chapter 4.

Chapter 4.

The Los Angeles Gas & Electric Co., 549 Aliso Street, Los Angeles.

Chapter 9.

Chapter 9.

Chapter 9.

Standard Oil Company, Baldwin Hills.

Chapter 8.

Chapter 8.

Chapter 8.

DAREDEVILS OF THE RED CIRCLE

Republic Studios backlot. All images are from Chapter 1.

Dick Tracy's G-Men
(1939)

Directors: William Witney and John English. **Cast:** Ralph Byrd (Dick Tracy), Irving Pichel (Nicolas Zarnoff), Ted Pearson (Steve Lockwood), Phylis Isley (Gwen Andrews), Walter Miller (Robal), George Douglas (Sandoval), Kenneth Harlan (Clive Anderson), Robert Carson (Scott), Julian Madison (Foster), Ted Mapes (Ted Murchison), William Stahl (Bruce), Robert Wayne (Wilbur), Joe McGuinn (Tom), Kenneth Terrell (Ed Hardy), Harry Humphrey (Stover), Harrison Greene (Baron).

Synopsis: International spy, Nicolas Zarnoff (**Irving Pichel**), in the employ of "The Three Powers" (presumably a fictionalized reference to the Axis) is captured by Dick Tracy (**Ralph Byrd**) at the start of the serial, tried and sentenced to death. However, through the use of a rare drug embedded by his agents in the evening newspaper, he escapes from the gas chamber. His men pick up his "corpse" by ambushing the hearse and administering another counter-drug. He continues his espionage plans, while taking the opportunity of revenge on Tracy.

Locations: Lower Iverson Ranch, Vasquez Rocks, Palmdale Area, Frank Meline Estate, 3636 Beverly Blvd, Alhambra Airport, Mountain Patrol #2, Morris Dam, Angelus Hangar at Metropolitan Airport, Los Angeles Angels Gate Lighthouse, White Point Hot Springs Hotel, Van Nuys City Hall, 14626 Ventura Blvd in Sherman Oaks, Lake Elsinore, Glendale Grand Central Air Terminal, probably Mormon Island, Republic Studio backlot, and stock shots of the FBI Field Office in San Francisco, L. A. Times Mirror Square building, and the Chatsworth Train Cut.

La Reina Theater, 14626 Ventura Blvd., Sherman Oaks (Chapter 1).

Grand Central Air Terminal, Glendale (Chapter 1).

Los Angeles Harbor Angels Gate Lighthouse (Chapter 3).

Angelus Hangar, Metropolitan Airport (Chapter 5).

Alhambra Airport opened in April 1930, and was located south of Valley Blvd. between New Avenue and Almansor Street in Alhambra (Chapter 9).

Palmdale area (Chapter 15).

The Chatsworth train cut in a mirror image of the actual look. This is a stock item (Chapter 5).

The Morris Dam is located in the San Gabriel Canyon adjacent to Highway 39. All three images on this page are from Chapter 6.

American Storage building, 3636 Beverly Blvd., Los Angeles.

The main entrance (Chapter 12).

While it looks like he is far up, he is barely past the first floor (Chapter 12).

The upper floors of the building (Chapter 12).

Lake Elsinore. All three images are from Chapter 1.

White Point Hot Springs Hotel appeared in Chapter 2 (all three images this page).

This lumber yard was probably on Mormon Island in Los Angeles Harbor. All three images are from Chapter 7).

Vasquez Rocks in Acton. All three images are from Chapter 15.

Mountain Patrol #2 was a small fire station and possibly a sheriff's sub-station located at 16500 Mulholland Drive. All three images from Chapter 7.

Lower Iverson Movie Ranch.

Chapter 12.

Chapter 6.

Chapter 6.

Republic Studio backlot.

New York Street (Chapter 1).

New York Street (Chapter 1).

New York Street (Chapter 2).

Republic Studio backlot.

New York Street (Chapter 8).

Western Street (Chapter 11).

Cantina Street (Chapter 11).

Zorro's Fighting Legion
(1939)

Directors: William Witney and John English. **Cast:** Reed Hadley (Zorro), Sheila Darcy (Volita), William Corson (Ramon), Leander de Cordova (Felipe), Edmund Cobb (Gonzales), John Merton (Manuel), C. Montague Shaw (Pablo), Budd Buster (Juan), Carleton Young (Benito Juarez), Guy D'Ennery (Don Francisco), Paul Marian (Kala), Joe Molina (Tarmac), Jim Pierce (Moreno), Helen Mitchel (Donna Maria), Curley Dresden (Tomas), Charles King (Valdez), Al Taylor (Rico).

Synopsis: The mysterious Don Del Oro ("Lord of Gold") (**C. Montague Shaw**), an idol of the Yaqui, emerges and attacks the gold trade of the Republic of Mexico, intent on becoming Emperor. A man named Francisco is put in charge of a fighting legion to combat the Yaqui tribe and protect the gold; he is attacked by men working for Don Del Oro. Francisco's partner recognizes Zorro as Don Diego Vega (**Reed Hadley**). Francisco asks Diego, as Zorro, to take over the fighting legion and defeat Don Del Oro.

Locations: Iverson Movie Ranch, Burro Flats, Republic Studio backlot.

Republic Studio backlot cave set (Chapter 1).

Three views of the Burro Flats located in the Santa Susana Mountains. All three images are from Chapter 2.

Three views of the Burro Flats located in the Santa Susana Mountains.

Chapter 2.

Chapter 2.

Chapter 5.

Iverson Movie Ranch.

Chapter 1.

Chapter 1.

Chapter 1.

Iverson Movie Ranch.

Chapter 1.

Chapter 3.

Chapter 6.

Iverson Movie Ranch.

Spanish Street (Chapter 11).

Hacienda Square (Chapter 2).

Spanish Street (Chapter 6).

Drums of Fu Manchu
(1940)

Directors: William Witney and John English. **Cast:** Henry Brandon (Fu Manchu), William Royle (Denis Nayland Smith), Robert Kellard (Allan Parker), Gloria Franklin (Fah-Lo-Suee), Olaf Hytten (Flinders Petrie), Tom Chatterton (Edward Randolph), Luana Walters (Mary Randolph), Lal Chand Mehra (Sirdar Prahni), George Cleveland (James Parker), John Dilson (Ezra Howard), John Merton (Loki), Dwight Frye (Anderson), Wheaton Chambers (Humphrey), George Pembroke (C. W. Crawford), Guy D'Ennery (Ranah Sang).

Synopsis: Fu Manchu (**Henry Brandon**) attempts to conquer the world by acquiring the sceptre of Genghis Khan, which will unite the people of Asia under his rule. Allan Parker (**Robert Kellard**) allies himself with the traditional British literary nemeses of Fu Manchu, Sir Denis Nayland Smith (**William Royle**) and his associate, Dr. Flinders Petrie (**Olaf Hytten**) after his father is kidnapped and killed by Fu Manchu's dacoits.

Locations: Iverson Movie Ranch, Lone Pine (stock), Corriganville, Lake Sherwood, Glendale Central Air Terminal, Radford Avenue bridge over L.A. River, Republic Studio front lot and backlot.

The Radford Avenue bridge over the Los Angeles River (Chapter 2).

The Grand Central Air Terminal in Glendale appeared in a sequence in Chapter 6.

Three views of Lake Sherwood (Chapter 11).

Corriganville Movie Ranch. Three views from Chapter 10.

The front entrance to the cave set.

The back entrance to the cave set, dressed with a door.

Corriganville Movie Ranch.

East of the cave set (Chapter 11).

Driving towards Robin Hood Forest (Chapter 11).

Robin Hood Forest. Up ahead, middle of the image, is the location of the lake which will be built in a few years (Chapter 11).

Iverson Movie Ranch.

Wee Willie Winkie sets (Chapter 13).

Lower Iverson (Chapter 14).

Upper Iverson (Chapter 11).

Republic Studio.

The Writers and Administration building on the front lot (Chapter 2).

Backlot New York Street (Chapter 2).

Backlot Cave Set (Chapter 10).

Adventures of Red Ryder (1940)

Directors: William Witney and John English. **Cast:** Don "Red" Barry (Red Ryder), Noah Beery (Ace Hanlon), Tommy Cook (Little Beaver), Maude Pierce Allen (The Duchess), Vivian Coe (Beth Andrews), Harry Worth (Calvin Drake), Hal Taliaferro (Cherokee Sims), William Farnum (Tom Ryder), Bob Kortman (One-Eye Chapin), Ray Teal (Shark), Gene Alsace (Lawson), Gayne Whitman (Harrison), Hooper Atchley (Treadway), John Dilson (Hale), Lloyd Ingraham (Luke Andrews), Charles Hutchinson (Brown), Gardner James (H. S. Barnett), Wheaton Chambers (Boswell), Lynton Brent (Len Clark).

Synopsis: The time is 1870 and Red Ryder (**Don Barry**), as the son of a rancher, Colonel Tom Ryder (**William Farnum**), is involved in the proceedings when his father is murdered by a gunmen of Ace Hanlon (**Noah Beery**), One-Eye Chapin (**Bob Kortman**), strong-arm man, saloon-keeper and stooge of the unscrupulous interests.

Locations: Iverson Ranch, Burro Flats, Lake Sherwood, Towsley Canyon (stock), and Republic Studio backlot and Los Angeles River.

Stock Footage of the Narrows at Towsley Canyon (episode 5).

ADVENTURES OF RED RYDER

Upper Iverson Ranch main chase road (episode 2).

Upper Iverson Ranch (episode 2).

Lake Sherwood (episode 2).

Three views of Burro Flats from episode 1.

Three views of Burro Flats.

Episode 1.

Episode 7.

Episode 7.

Republic Studio Backlot.

Western Street (episode 1).

This barn was located just to the east of where the future Duchess Ranch was built in 1943 for the Red Ryder series. It did not survive (episode 5).

Western Street (episode 1).

Republic Studio Backlot.

These sets were removed by 1941 (episode 2).

Western Street (episode 2).

Los Angeles River that passed through the Republic Studio property (episode 10).

King of the Royal Mounted (1940)

Directors: William Witney and John English. **Cast:** Allan Lane (Dave King), Robert Strange (John Kettler), Robert Kellard (Tom Merritt Jr.), Lita Conway (Linda Merritt), Herbert Rawlinson (Ross King), Harry Cording (Wade Garson), Bryant Washburn (Matt Crandall), Budd Buster (Vinegar Smith), Stanley Andrews (Tom Merritt Sr.), John Davidson (Shelton), John Dilson (Wall), Paul McVey (Zarnoff), Lucien Prival (Johnson), Norman Willis (Tarner), Tony Paton (LeCouteau).

Synopsis: In World War II, the Nazis require a special mineral, Compound X, discovered in Canada. Although intended to cure paralysis, the Nazis have discovered that it can be used in magnetic mines to destroy the British fleet and blockade America to prevent it assisting the Allies. The Mounties discover this plot and work to defeat and capture the Nazi spies sent to obtain the ore. Sgt King's father (**Herbert Rawlinson**) is killed in the line of duty, saving his son, Sergeant Dave King (**Allan Lane**), from death on a circular saw, and leaving him to carry on the fight against the enemy.

Locations: Big Bear, Cedar Lake, Chatsworth Train Tunnel #1, and Republic Studio backlot.

Chatsworth Train Tunnel #1 (Santa Susanna Road overpass (Chapter 5).

KING OF THE ROYAL MOUNTED

Cedar Lake at Big Bear was originally known as Bartlett Lake when the dam was built to create the lake. It was later renamed Cedar Lake. Most of the sets at the lake were built for the 1936 film *Trail of the Lonesome Pine*. Because of safety issues, the mill at the dam was torn down in the 1990's and a replica erected in its place. (Chapter 2).

Chapter 11.

Chapter 11.

The dam at Big Bear Lake. All three images are from Chapter 9.

The *Brigham Young* film sets at Big Bear.

Chapter 1.

Chapter 1.

The only surviving Brigham Young set at Big Bear.

Big Bear and Big Bear Lake.

Chapter 1.

Chapter 2.

Chapter 4.

KING OF THE ROYAL MOUNTED

Republic Studio Backlot.

The backlot cave set (Chapter 8).

Backlot lagoon (Chapter 1).

Backlot lagoon (Chapter1).

Mysterious Doctor Satan
(1940)

Directors: William Witney and John English. **Cast:** Edward Ciannelli (Doctor Satan), Robert Wilcox (Bob Wayne), William Newell (Speed Martin), C. Montague Shaw (Thomas Scott), Ella Neal (Lois Scott), Dorothy Herbert (Alice Brent), Charles Trowbridge (Bronson), Jack Mulhall (Rand), Edwin Stanley (Bevans), Walter McGrail (Stoner), Joe McGuinn (Gort), Bud Geary (Hallett), Paul Marion (Corbay), Archie Twitchell (Ross), Lynton Brent (Scarlett), Kenneth Terrell (Corwin), Al Taylor (Joe).

Synopsis: Governor Bronson (**Charles Trowbridge**), who raised Bob Wayne (**Robert Wilcox**) from childhood after the death of his parents, is killed at the hands of a world-domination-seeking mad scientist called Doctor Satan (**Edward Ciannelli**). Fearing his death might be at hand, as it has been for everyone else who had opposed the Doctor, the Governor first confides in Wayne with a secret about his past. Bob's father was really an outlaw in the Old West, who fought injustice while wearing a chainmail cowl and leaving small coiled copper snakes as his calling card. Following his guardian's death, Wayne decides to adopt his father's Copperhead persona and cowl. Doctor Satan, meanwhile, requires only a remote control device invented by Professor Scott to complete his army of killer robots and gain all the power and riches he desires.

Locations: Iverson Movie Ranch, Stearns Wharf, 3636 Beverly Blvd, 1103 Celis St., Albert B Schoen Gas Station, Hotel Goodhap, Trading Post, Chatsworth Depot, L.A. Gas and Electric Co., Forest Lawn Drive (stock), White Point Beach, and Republic Studio front lot and backlot.

Sterling Electric Co., 1103 Celis Street, San Fernando (Chapter 5).

The White Point Hot Springs Hotel and Restaurant as seen in Chapter 14.

Three views of the City of San Fernando.

Hotel Goodhap, 208 S. Brand Blvd. (Chapter 8).

The building to the left of the Hotel Goodhap (Chapter 8).

The building on the near corner, 218 S. Brand Blvd., was for businesses such as Dr. John J. Brooks, Optometrist (Chapter 8).

Trading Post, 810 San Fernando Road, San Fernando (Chapter 8).

Turning the corner from San Fernando Road onto Chatsworth Drive, San Fernando (Chapter 8).

Albert B. Schoen Gas Station on the corner, 216 S. Maclay Ave., San Fernando (Chapter 5).

Iverson Movie Ranch. All three images are from Chapter 8.

MYSTERIOUS DOCTOR SATAN

The Los Angeles Gas and Electric Company. All three images are from Chapter 10.

Stearns Wharf, Santa Barbara. All three images are from Chapter 1.

American Storage building, 3636 Beverly Blvd., Los Angeles.

Chapter 3. This is the south side of the building where historically there was a parking lot. That lot is now gone.

A view of the side of the building (Chapter 3).

A view from the top of the building looking down on Westmoreland Ave. The building in the lower right is still there (Chapter 3).

Chatsworth Train Depot (Chapter 8).

Chatsworth Train Depot (Chapter 8).

Angelus Hangar, Metropolitan Airport (Chapter 2).

MYSTERIOUS DOCTOR SATAN

Republic Studio Backlot.

The miniature pool (Chapter 3).

The miniature pool (Chapter 5).

Cave set (Chapter 9).

Adventures of Captain Marvel (1941)

Directors: William Witney and John English. **Cast:** Tom Tyler (Captain Marvel), Frank Coghlan, Jr. (Billy Batson), William Benedict (Whitey Murphy), Louise Currie (Betty Wallace), Robert Strange (John Malcolm), Harry Worth (Luther Bentley), Bryant Washburn (Henry Carlyle), John Davidson (Tal Chotali), George Pembroke (Stephen Lang), Peter George Lynn (Dwight Fisher), Reed Hadley (Rahman Bar), Jack Mulhall (James Howell), Kenneth Duncan (Barnett), Nigel de Brulier (Shazam), John Bagni (Cowan), Carleton Young (Martin), Leland Hodgson (Rawley), Stanley Price (Owens), Ernest Sarracino (Akbar), Tetsu Komai (Chan Lal).

Synopsis: Captain Marvel (**Tom Tyler**), who by special power is invincible and able to overcome all dangers and obstacles. The story concerns an expedition to a remote section of Siam seeking knowledge of an ancient Scorpion Dynasty. The expedition uncovers a complicated series of lenses which, properly focused, turns any solid object to gold. The lenses are divided among members of the party so that no one of them will have sole possession.

Locations: Iverson Movie Ranch, Max Whittier Estate, Lake Sherwood, Bronson Canyon Cave, Eight & Normandie Garage, Republic Studio backlot.

Lower Iverson Movie Ranch (Chapter 1).

Apartment building at 1975 N. Beachwood Drive. Front Entrance (Chapter 5).

Back entrance on Gower Street (Chapter 2).

Radford Avenue Bridge over the Los Angeles River near to the studio. Camera is facing northeast (Chapter 3).

Lake Sherwood and Sherwood Forest area.

Cliff overlooking Lake Sherwood (Chapter 7).

Southeastern side of the lake (Chapter 7).

At the bottom of the dam (Chapter 7).

Lake Sherwood Dam. All three images are from Chapter 7. **NOTE:** See how the actors are staying close to the lake side of the dam? The other side is a long drop and could easily result in death from a fall off the top.

The Max Whittier Estate, 9561 Sunset Blvd at Alpine Drive. All three images are from Chapter 8. The original house is no longer having been torn down with a more modern mansion erected in its place.

ADVENTURES OF CAPTAIN MARVEL

The Eight & Normandie Garage, 761 S. Normandie Ave.

A view of the entrance (Chapter 5).

Captain Marvel (Tom Tyler) looking up at the building (Chapter 5).

Captain Marvel (the balsa wood dummy) "flying up" the front of the building (Chapter 5).

The Cafe at 12001 Ventura Place, at the corner of Radford Avenue, was owned by Thomas F. Rogers. A demolition application is dated July 11, 1941. This is the Radford Avenue side (Chapter 3). The building to the right of the alley is still there.

The alley which ran on the north side of the cafe, looking east (Chapter 3).

Coldwater Canyon and Mulholland Drive (Chapter 3).

ADVENTURES OF CAPTAIN MARVEL

Bronson Canyon Cave. This is the "Phantom Empire" entrance, the right most one on the inside portion of the canyon, two others to the left (Chapter 5).

Entering the cave (Chapter 5).

Now appearing at the Republic Studio cave set on the backlot (Chapter 5).

The Lower Iverson Movie Ranch.

Chapter 1.

Chapter 1.

Chapter 1.

ADVENTURES OF CAPTAIN MARVEL

The Lower Iverson Movie Ranch.

Chapter 11.

Chapter 11.

Republic Studio Backlot.

New York Street (Chapter 3).

New York Street (Chapter 5).

Spanish Street (Chapter 11).

Jungle Girl
(1941)

Directors: William Witney and John English. **Cast:** Frances Gifford (Nyoka Meredith), Tom Neal (Jack Stanton), Trevor Bardette (Bradley Meredith), Gerald Mohr (Slick Latimer), Eddie Acuff (Curly Rogers), Frank Lackteen (Shamba), Tommy Cook (Kimbu), Robert Barron (Bombo), Al Kikume (Lutembi), Bud Geary (Brock), Al Taylor (Claggett), Joe McGuinn (Ted Bone), Jerry Frank (Lion Chief), Kenneth Terrell (Mananga).

Synopsis: Dr. John Meredith (**Trevor Bardette**), ashamed at the crime spree of his evil twin brother, Bradley (**Trevor Bardette**), travels with his daughter, Nyoka Meredith (**Frances Gifford**), to Africa. There his skills as a doctor displace Shamba (**Frank Lackteen**), the resident witch doctor of the Masamba. Years later, Slick Latimer (**Gerald Mohr**) and Bradley Meredith arrive looking for a local diamond mine and team up with the disgruntled Shamba. Bradley kills his brother John and takes his place. They also bring along Jack Stanton (**Tom Neal**) and Curly Rogers (**Eddie Acuff**), who promptly join Nyoka in trying to stop the villains.

Locations: Iverson Movie Ranch, Corriganville, Lake Sherwood and Sherwood Forest, Republic Studio backlot and Los Angeles River.

Republic Studios backlot cave set (Chapter 2).

Three views of the Sherwood Forest area as seen in Chapter 1.

Lake Sherwood diving cliff (Chapter 1).

Republic Studio backlot Underwater Tank (Chapter 1).

Republic Studio backlot Los Angeles River (Chapter 7).

Three views of the Lower Iverson Movie Ranch in the Gorge area (all images from Chapter 11)

Corriganville Movie Ranch.

Robin Hood Forest heading towards the cave set (Chapter 1).

A newly dressed entrance to the cave set (Chapter 1).

Looking down from a perch on the ranch (Chapter 1).

Corriganville Movie Ranch.

Chapter 6.

Chapter 7.

Chapter 9.

Republic Studios backlot Native Village.

Chapter 1.

Chapter 1.

Chapter 8.

King of the Texas Rangers (1941)

Directors: William Witney and John English. **Cast:** "Slingin' Sammy" Baugh (Tom King Jr), Neil Hamilton (John Barton), Pauline Moore (Sally Crane), Duncan Renaldo (Pedro Garcia), Charles Trowbridge (Robert Crawford), Herbert Ralinson (Lee Avery), Frank Darien (Pop Evans), Robert O. Davis (His Excellency), Monte Blue (Tom J. King Sr), Stanley Blystone (A. J. Lynch), Kermit Maynard (Wichita Bates), Roy Barcroft (Ross), Kenneth Duncan (Nick), Jack Ingram (Shorty), Robert Barron (Blake), Frank Bruno (Cole), Monte Montague (Dade), Joseph Forte (Nelson), Lucien Prival (Captain).

Synopsis: Captain Tom J. King (**Monte Blue**) of the Texas Rangers is murdered after he has learned that John Barton (**Neil Hamilton**), supposedly a respectable citizen, and "His Excellency" (**Rudolph Anders**), a mysterious alien, are the leaders of a sabotage gang engaged in destroying the Bordertown oil fields. His son, Tom King (**"Slingin' Sammy Baugh"**), a famous football player, joins the Rangers, eager to avenge his father's death.

Locations: Iverson Movie Ranch, Brandeis Ranch, Lake Sherwood, Baldwin Hills Oil Field, Chatsworth Train Cut (stock), Chatsworth Train Tunnel #1, Miner Street Wharf, near Palmdale, Adams Port, Morris Dam, old San Gabriel Canyon Road, Republic Studio backlot.

Adams Port (Chapter 5).

Baldwin Hills Oil Fields.

Chapter 1.

Chapter 1.

Chapter 3.

Lake Sherwood.

Chapter 7.

Chapter 9.

Brandeis Ranch (Chapter 4).

Morris Dam, located in San Gabriel Canyon alongside Highway 39. All three images are from Chapter 10.

Corriganville Movie Ranch.

All three images are from Chapter 9.

Lower Iverson Movie Ranch.

Chapter 1.

Chapter 2

Chapter 2.

The Lower Iverson Movie Ranch

The Gorge Cabin and Devil's Gateway (Chapter 4).

The Devil's Gateway (Chapter 4).

The meadow (Chapter 4).

Miner Street Wharf, San Pedro. All three images are from Chapter 3.

Forest Lawn Drive, Burbank (Chapter 3).

West side tunnel view of the Chatsworth train line (Chapter 2).

An unidentified ranch (Chapter 6).

Republic Studio backlot

Hacienda Square (Chapter 9).

Cantina Street (Chapter 9).

The soon-to-be-gone barn set, redressed as Rangers Headquarters (Chapter 4).

Republic Studio Backlot.

Western Street (Chapter 1).

Western Street (Chapter 1).

Backlot cave set (Chapter 4).

Dick Travy vs. Crime, Inc. (1941)

Directors: William Witney and John English. **Cast:** Ralph Byrd (Dick Tracy), Michael Owen (Bill Carr), Jan Wiley (June Chandler), John Davidson (Lucifer), Ralph Morgan (J. P. Morton), Kenneth Harlan (Cosgrove), John Dilson (Henry Weldon), Howard HIckman (Stephen Chandler), Robert Frazer (Daniel Brewster), Robert Fiske (Walter Cabot), Jack Mulhall (Jim Wilson), Hooper Alchley (Arthur Trent), Anthony Warde (John Corey), Chuck Morrison (Trask).

Synopsis: Dick Tracy (**Ralph Byrd**) is sent from Washington to track down a notorious criminal known as The Ghost—one of eight noted individuals who comprise a committee for "crime prevention".

Locations: Iverson Movie Ranch, Van Nuys City Hall, Lake Elsinore, San Pedro Harbor, Royal Palms Beach, Burton Green Estate, Chatsworth Depot, Republic Studio backlot.

Royal Palms Beach (Chapter 2).

Three views of the Chatsworth Train Depot. All images are from Chapter 3.

The Burton Green Estate, 1601 Lexington Road, Beverly Hills (Chapter 1).

The front gate to the estate. While the gateway is no longer there, the two posts are (Chapter 1).

Van Nuys Police Station (Chapter 2).

Three views of San Pedro Harbor.

Chapter 5.

Chapter 5.

Chapter 6.

At the far end of the image is the Southland Music Co., 6265 Van Nuys Blvd., Van Nuys (Chapter 14).

Van Nuys Fire Station, 14415 Sylvan Street, Van Nuys (Chapter 14).

At the rea of the Van Nuys City Hall (Chapter 14).

Second unit or stock shot of the old Cedars of Lebanon Hospital. It is now owned by Scientology (Chapter 15).

Stock shot of the old Hollywood Fire Department builing on Cahuenga (Chapter 10).

Stock shot of the Mountain Patrol #2 location on Mulholland Drive (Chapter 6).

The entrance to the Lower Iverson Movie Ranch off of Santa Suanna Pass Road (Chapter 11).

Lower Iverson Movie Ranch (Chapter 11).

Lower Iverson Movie Ranch (Chapter 11).

Republic Studio Backlot

New York Street.
Chapter 1.

New York Street.
Chapter 3.

Melody Ranch Barn.
Chapter 8.

Republic Studios backlot alley between Western Street to the north and New York Square to the south (Chapter 10).

The incinerator on the backlot south of New York Street (Chapter 11).

Interior of one of the non-sound stages on the lot (Chapter 11).

Spy Smasher
(1942)

Director: William Witney. **Cast:** Kane Richmond (Spy Smasher), Marguerite Chapman (Eve Corby), Sam Flint (Corby), Hans Schumm (The Mask), Tristram Coffin (Drake), Franco Corsaro (Pierre Durand), Hans Von Morhart (Gerhardt), Georges Renavent (LeConte), Robert O. Davis (Von Kahr), Henry Zynda (Ritter Lazar), Paul Bryar (Lawlor), Tom London (Crane), Richard Bond (Hayes), Crane Whitley (Hauser), John James (Steve).

Synopsis: Spy Smasher (**Kane Richmond**), mysterious American free-lance agent in occupied France, is captured by the Germans while attempting to get information about The Mask (**Hans Schumm**), head of the German spy ring in America. He is sentenced to the firing squad, but Pierre Durand (**Franco Corsaro**), a loyal Free Frenchman, saves him and arranges his escape to America. In America, he contacts his twin brother, Jack, and enlists his aid in fighting their common enemy. The brothers learn that The Mask is planning an attack on Admiral Corby (**Sam Flint**), head of the U. S. Foreign Service and father of Jack's fiancee, Eve (**Marguerite Chapman**).

Locations: Iverson Movie Ranch, Lake Elsinore and Showboat Restaurant, Taylor Ranch Lake Elsinore, Los Angeles Brick and Clay Products, Alberhill (now Pacific Clay Products), Alberhill Post Office, 12323 Sherman Way, Republic Studio backlot.

The Alberhill Post Office Building and Restaurant (Chapter 10).

The Showboat Restaurant at Lake. The boat was mounted on wheels on a rail system and could be lowered into the lake water. Chapter 12.

Spy Smasher's stunt double diving into Lake Elsinore from the Showboat Restaurant (Chapter 12).

The Showboat Restaurant out of the water near the end of its life.

The Sherman Way underpass for the Pacific Electric Train tracks (Chapter 9).

Fillmore Cement Products, 12323 Sherman Way, North Hollywood (Chapter 9).

Fillmore Cement Products, 12323 Sherman Way, North Hollywood (Chapter 9).

Lake Elsinore, near Mohr Street and Lakeshore Drive (Chapter 1).

Lake Elsinore, Chapter 1.

Radford Avenue bridge over the Los Angeles River next to Republic Studio (Chapter 8).

Los Angeles Brick and Clay Company, Alberhill.

Chapter 10.

Chapter 10.

Chapter 10.

SPY SMASHER 189

The city of Alberhill housed the workers at the clay tile plant (Chapter 10).

Alberhill (Chapter 10).

A view of the clay plant (Chapter 10).

Iverson Movie Ranch.

Chapter 7.

Chapter 4.

Chapter 9.

Republic Studio backlot.

Hacienda Square (Chapter 2).

Melody Ranch barn (Chapter 3)..

New York Street (Chapter 5).

Perils of Nyoka
(1942)

Director: William Witney. **Cast:** Kay Aldridge (Nyoka Gordon), Clayton Moore (Larry Grayson), William Benedict (Red Davis), Lorna Gray (Vultura), Charles Middleton (Cassib), Tristram Coffin (Benito Torini), Forbes Murray (Douglas Campbell), Robert Strange (Henry Gordon), George Pembroke (John Spencer), George Renavent (Maghreb), John Davidson (Lhoba), George LEwis (Batan), Ken Terrell (Ahmed), John Bagni (Ben Ali), Kenneth Duncan (Abou), Arvon Dale (Bedouin 1).

Synopsis: It starts off with an archeologist's expedition to the Arabian desert to find an ancient papyrus giving instructions for finding the lost Tablets of Hippocrates, with Nyoka Gordon (**Kay Aldridge**) living with a Bedouin tribe, the only person able to decipher it. She is hunting for her missing father, Professor Henry Gordon (**Robert Strange**). Vultura (**Lorna Gray**), exotic ruler of a band of vicious Arabs, is determined to get the Tablets and the treasure hidden with them, and steals the papyrus before Nyoka joins the expedition.

Locations: Iverson Movie Ranch, Corriganville, Republic Studio backlot.

Republic Studio backlot cave set (Chapter 1).

PERILS OF NYOKA

Corriganville Movie Ranch—three views.

The future site of the Robin Hood Lake (Chapter 1).

Chapter 1.

Chapter 1.

The Corriganville Movie Ranch cave (Chapter 5).

One of the Iverson Movie Ranch caves (Chapter 4).

The Garden of the Gods at the Iverson Movie Ranch (Chapter 1).

Iverson Movie Ranch

Vultura's Palace (a false front between two rock formations) (Chapter 1).

A scenic view of the lower Iverson towards the Nyoka Cliff (Chapter 1).

Ivereson Devil's Gateway in the background (Chapter 1).

Lower Iverson Movie Ranch

Nyoka Cliff (Chapter 7).

Lower Iverson Movie Ranch. Atop the Nyoka Cliff (Chapter 7).

Republic Studio backlot, Cantina Street (Chapter 1).

King of the Mounties
(1942)

Director: William Witney. **Cast:** Allan Lane (Dave King), Gilbert Emery (Morrison), Russell Hicks (Carleton), Peggy Drake (Carol Brent), George Irving (Marshall Brent), Abner Biberman (Yamata), William Vaughn (Von Horst), Nestor Paiva (Baroni), Bradley Page (Charles Blake), Douglass Dumbrille (Gil Harper), William Bakewell (Hall Ross), Duncan Renaldo (Pierre), Francis Ford (Zeke Collins), Jay Novello (Lewis), Anthony Warde (Stark), Norman Nesbitt (Newscaster), John Hiestand (Lane), Allen Jung (Sato), Paul Fung (Bombardier), Arvon Dale (Craig).

Synopsis: Canada is being bombed mercilessly by a mysterious plane, which is shaped like a boomerang, and is dubbed the Falcon. The plane is under the command of Japanese admiral Yamata (**Abner Biberman**). The identity of the plane remains a mystery until Professor Marshall Brent (**George Irving**) and his daughter Carol (**Peggy Drake**) arrive with a new type of airplane detector. The Axis forces are planning a Canadian invasion, and feeling that Professor Brent poses a threat to their plan, they kidnap him. RCMP Sergeant Dave King (**Allan Lane**) attempts a rescue, but the professor is killed when the plane in which he is held captive crashes into a riverboat.

Locations: Lower Iverson Ranch (stock), Big Bear, Cedar Lake, Saugus Train Depot (stock), Chatsworth Train Tunnel #1 (stock), Republic Studio backlot.

Brigham Young movie set at Big Bear (Chapter 7).

Three views of Cedar Lake.

Chapter 1.

Chapter 1.

Chapter 5.

KING OF THE MOUNTIES

Three views of Big Bear Lake.

Chapter 1.

Chapter 1.

Chapter 9.

Three views of Big Bear Lake and vicinity.

Chapter 9.

Chapter 5.

Chapter 2.

Three views of Big Bear.

Chapter 1.

Chapter 1.

Chapter 2.

G-Men vs. the Black Dragon (1942)

Director: William Witney. **Cast:** Rod Cameron (Rex Bennett), Roland Got (Chang Sing), Constance Worth (Vivian Marsh), Nino Pipitone (Oyama Haruchi), Noel Cravat (Ranga), George Lewis (Lugo), Maxine Doyle (Marie), Donald Kirke (Muller), Ivan Miller (Customs Inspector), Walter Fenner (Williams), C. Montague Shaw (Nicholson), Harry Burns (Tony Mills), Forbes Murray (James Kennedy), Hooper Atchley (Harrison J. Caldwell), Robert HOmas (Gorman), Allen Jung (Fuji).

Synopsis: After Japanese spies from the Black Dragon Society infiltrate United States borders, Federal Agent Rex Bennett (**Rod Cameron**) is enlisted by the government to capture them. As Oyama Haruchi (**Nino Pipitone**), leader of the dangerous paramilitary group, begins to destabilize the United States war effort through sabotage and corruption, Bennett must team up with British special agent Vivian Marsh (**Constance Worth**) and Chinese special agent Chang Sing (**Roland Got**) to stop them and help win the war.

Locations: Stearns Wharf, Adams Port, Casa Dorinda, Republic Studio backlot.

Casa Dorinda, Montecito (Chapter 12).

Three views of the Stearns Wharf area in Santa Barbara. All images are from Chapter 9.

Adams Port (Chapter 5).

Adams Port (Chapter 5).

Unidentified location (Chapter 14).

Republic Studios backlot.

New York Street (Chapter 1).

Western Street (Chapter 6).

Western Street (Chapter 6).

Daredevils of the West (1943)

Director: John English. **Cast:** Allan Lane (Duke Cameron), Kay Aldridge (June Foster), Eddie Acuff (Red Kelly), William Haade (Barton Ward), Robert Frazer (Martin Dexter), Ted Adams (Silas Higby), George Lewis (Turner), Stanley Andrews (Andrews), Jack Rockwell (Watson), Charles Miller (Foster), John Hamilton (Garfield), Budd Buster (Jim Brady), Kenneth Harlan (Commissioner), Rex Lease (Jack), Chief Thundercloud (Indian Chief).

Synopsis: Story concerns the efforts of June Foster (**Kay Aldridge**), daughter of a murdered stage line operator (**Charles Miller**), who is fighting to carry through her father's plans for running a road into the Comanche Strip.

Locations: Iverson Movie Ranch, Lone Pine, Republic Studio backlot.

Republic Studio backlot cave set (Chapter 4).

DAREDEVILS OF THE WEST

Three views of the Iverson Movie Ranch.

On top of the overlook cliff opposite of the Nyoka Cliff and behind the Garden of the Gods (Chapter 3).

A view of the Upper Iverson (Chapter 6).

Chapter 2.

Lone Pine, Alabama Hills (Chapter 1).

Lone Pine, Alabama Hills (Chapter 1).

Lone Pine, Alabama Hills (Chapter 1).

DAREDEVILS OF THE WEST

Lone Pine, Alabama Hills (Chapter 4).

Lone Pine, Alabama Hills (Chapter 5).

Lone Pine, Alabama Hills (Chapter 1).

Republic Studio backlot.

Melody Ranch barn (Chapter 8).

Western Street (Chapter 1.

Brazos Street (Chapter 3).

Secret Service in Darkest Africa (1943)

Director: Spencer Bennet. **Cast:** Rod Cameron (Rex Bennett), Joan Marsh (Janet Blake), Duncan Renaldo (Pierre LaSalle), Lionel Royce (Abou Ben Ali), Lionel Royce (Von Rommler), Kurt Krueger (Ernst Muller), Frederic Brunn (Wolfe), Sigurd Tor (Luger), George Renavent (Armand), Kurt Katch (Kurt Hauptman), Ralf Harolde (Captain), William Vaughn (Boschert), William Yetter (Commandant), Hans Von Morhart (Sub Officer), Erwin Goldi (Von Raeder), Frederic Worlock (James Langley).

Synopsis: In an attempt to control the entire Middle East and defeat the Allies, Nazi agent Baron von Rommler (**Lionel Royce**) captures and impersonates Sultan Abou Ben Ali (also **Lionel Royce**), leader of all the Arabs. Opposed to him is Secret Service Agent Rex Bennett (**Rod Cameron**), along with British reporter Janet Blake (**Joan Marsh**) and Chief of Police Captain Pierre LaSalle (**Duncan Renaldo**).

Locations: Iverson Movie Ranch, Lake Elsinore, Republic Studio backlot.

The Showboat Restaurant at Lake Elsinore (Chapter 1).

Three views of Lake Elsinore.

Chapter 8.

Chapter 3.

Chapter 1.

SECRET SERVICE IN DARKEST AFRICA

Three Views of the Iverson Movie Ranch.

Chapter 3.

Chapter 2.

Chapter 2.

Three Views of the Iverson Movie Ranch.

Chapter 8.

Chapter 9.

Chapter 11.

The Republic Studio lot.

Cantina Street on the backlot (Chapter 1).

Front lot buildings (Chapter 1).

New York Street (Chapter 8).

The Masked Marvel
(1943)

Director: Spencer Bennet. **Cast:** William Forrest (Martin Crane), Louise Currie (Alice Hamilton), Johnny Arthur (Mura Sakima), Rod Bacon (Jim Arnold), Richard Clarke (Frank Jeffers), David Bacon (Bob Barton), Bill Healy (Terry Morton), Howard HIckman (Warren Hamilton), Kenneth Harlan (Plant Guard), Thomas Louden (Mathews), Eddie Parker (Meggs), Duke Green (Karl), Dale Van Sickel (Kline), Wendell Niles (Newscaster), Lester Dorr (Reporter 1).

Synopsis: In The Masked Marvel (**David Bacon**), a hero dressed in a business suit and a face mask fights the Japanese saboteur Mura Sakima (**Johnny Arthur**) and his espionage organization. The hook of the story is that, in a reversal of the common serial "Masked Mystery Villain" stock character, the audience doesn't know who the hero is until the final reel—all the audience is told is that The Masked Marvel is one of a group of special investigators.

Locations: Chatsworth Train Depot, Stearns Wharf, Casa Dorinda, Santa Barbara, Van Nuys City Hall, The Harbor Restaurant, Republic Studio backlot.

Unidentified Signal Oil Gas Station (episode 3).

THE MASKED MARVEL

Two views of Casa Dorinda in Montecito.

Front View (episode 3).

Back View (episode 1).

The group standing in front of the Marine Cafe—location unidentified (episode 6).

Chatsworth Train Depot. Three views of the location from episode 10.

THE MASKED MARVEL

The Harbor Restaurant on Stearns Wharf in Santa Barbara. It was originally the Santa Barbara Yacht Club, beginning in 1926. In 1941, Ronald Coleman and Senator Alvin Weingand purchased it and converted it into a restaurant. In 1981, it was completely rebuilt by the third set of owners.

Episode 2

Episode 2

Vintage image of the restaurant.

Stearns Wharf, Santa Barbara.

Episode 6.

Episode 6.

Episode 2.

Republic Studios backlot.

New York Street (episode 7).

False front building near the miniature pool (episode 6.)

Outside a front lot building (episode 1).

Captain America
(1944)

Directors: John English and Elmer Clifton. **Cast:** Dick Purcell (Captain America/Grant Gardner), Lorna Gray (Gail Richards), Lionel Atwill (Cyrus Maldor), Charles Trowbridge (Dryden), Russell Hicks (Randolph), George J. Lewis (Bart Matson), John Davidson (Gruber), Norman Nesbitt (Newscaster), Frank Reicher (Lyman), Hugh Sothern (Eldon Dodge), Tom Chatterton (J. C. Henley), Robert Frazer (Clinton Lyman), John Hamilton (G. F. Hillman), Crane Whitley (Dirk), Edward Keane (Agent 33), John Bagni (Monk), Jay Novello (Simms).

Synopsis: A rash of suspicious suicides among scientists and businessmen, all found holding a small scarab, gets the attention of Mayor Randolph (**Russell Hicks**). He demands that Police Commissioner Dryden (**Charles Trowbridge**) and District Attorney Grant Gardner (**Dick Purcell**) get to the bottom of the case, while openly wishing that Captain America (**Dick Purcell**), a masked man who has helped defeat crime in the past, were around to solve the mystery. Gail Richards (**Lorna Gray**), Grant Gardner's secretary, investigates and realizes someone knows of the "Purple Death", a hypnotic chemical responsible for the suicides.

Locations: Van Nuys City Hall, 1314 N Haywood Ave, 500 S Westmoreland, 12003 Ventura Blvd., Iverson Movie Ranch, Republic Studio backlot and front lot.

John C. Mehan Inc. Used Cars, 12003 Ventura Blvd., Studio City (Chapter 7).

Lower Iverson Movie Ranch

The car is on the Stagecoach Road which traveled around the base of the Nyoka Cliff. Rifleman is perched atop an overlook directly behind (south side) of the Garden of the Gods (Chapter 6).

Badman George J. Lewis heads to the dropoff spot (Chapter 6).

Captain America drives away from the overlook, through the Garden of the Gods. Unbenownst to everyone, there is a movie set out in the flat from some other film (Chapter 6).

Casa Bonita Apartments, 500 S. Westmoreland Ave., Los Angeles. All three views from Chapter 9.

Main entrance on Westmoreland Ave.

The corner of the apartments at Westmoreland Ave. and 5th Street.

The 5th Street side.

The Haywood Tower, 1314 N. Haywood Ave., West Hollywood.

The entrance (Chapter 3).

Looking down to the sidewalk (Chapter 3).

The bad guys exiting the property. Across the street is 1313 N. Haywood and that building still stands (Chapter 8).

Van Nuys City Hall.

Front entrance to City Hall (Chapter 2).

Wider view of the City Hall building (Chapter 9).

Republic Studio backlot, Melody Ranch barn (Chapter 9).

Tiger Woman
(1944)

Directors: Spencer Bennet and Wallace Grissell. **Cast:** Allan Lane (Allen Saunders), Linda Stirling (The Tiger Woman), Duncan Renaldo (Jose Delgado), George J. Lewis (Morgan), LeRoy Mason (Fletcher Walton), Crane Whitley (Tom Dagget), Robert Frazer (Ramgah), Rico de Montez (Tegula), Stanley Price (Mac), Nolan Leary (Scott), Kenne Duncan (Gentry), Tom Steele (Temple Heavy 1), Duke Greene (Flint), Eddie Parker (Travis), Ken Terrell (Bolton), Cliff Lyons (Rand).

Synopsis: The Tiger Woman/Rita Arnold (**Linda Stirling**) is a female white Tarzan whose Indian subjects conduct sadistic death dances before they boil their victims in burning oil.

Locations: Iverson Movie Ranch, Sherwood Forest (stock), Lake Elsinore, Republic Studio backlot.

Republic Studio backlot Western Street redressed for Africa plus a matte painting for the top third of the frame (Chapter 1).

Three views of Lake Elsinore (Chapter 9).

TIGER WOMAN

Lower Iverson Movie Ranch.

Garden of the Gods (Chapter 2).

Chapter 1.

Chapter 1.

Lower Iverson Movie Ranch.

Chapter 2.

Chapter 3.

Chapter 1.

Haunted Harbor
(1944)

Directors: Spencer Bennet and Wallace Grissell. **Cast:** Kane Richmond (Jim Marsden), Kay Aldridge (Patricia Harding), Roy Barcroft (Carter), Clancy Cooper (Yank), Marshall Reed (Tommy), Oscar O'Shea (John Galbraith), Forrest Taylor (Oliver Harding), Hal Taliafero (Lawson), Edward Keane (Fredrick Vorhees), George J. Lewis (Dranga), Kenne Duncan (Gregg), Bud Geary (Snell), Robert Homans (Port Captain), Duke Green (Neville), Dale Van Sickel (Duff), Tom Steele (Ronson), Rico de Montez (Tamil).

Synopsis: Sea captain Jim Marsden (**Kane Richmond**) is about to be hanged for a murder he didn't commit, and is rescued from the gallows by two of his crewmen. To clear the captain's name, they head for the island of Pulinan, where they believe the real murderer is hiding. During the search for the killer, one thing leads to another and Jim and the crew soon find that their troubles have just started. Investigating a possible hiding place of the killer, Jim encounters huge sea monsters in *Haunted Harbor*.

Locations: Iverson Movie Ranch, Lake Sherwood, Republic Studio backlot.

Lake Sherwood (Chapter 5).

Three views of the Iverson Movie Ranch.

Chapter 2.

Chapter 3.

Chapter 7.

HAUNTED HARBOR

Lower Iverson Movie Ranch.

Nyoka Cliff (Chapter 3).

On top of Nyoka Cliff (Chapter 3).

Garden of the Gods partially seen to the far right (Chapter 2).

Republic Studio backlot. Chapter 2.

Chapter 3.

Entering the cave entrance in the artificial hill on the backlot. Chapter 1.

HAUNTED HARBOR

Republic Studio backlot.

Chapter 6.

Chapter 12.

Chapter 10.

Republic Studio backlot.

The monster in the lagoon (a portion of the artificial hill is in the background. Chapter 5.

Fighting on the side of the hill that separated the main lot from the lower portion. Chapter 5.

The backlot cave set (Chapter 3.

Zorro's Black Whip
(1944)

Directors: Spencer Bennet and Wallace Grissell. **Cast:** George J. Lewis (Vic Gordon), Linda Stirling (Barbara Meredith), Lucien Littlefield (Tenpoint Jackson), Francis McDonald (Dan Hammond), Hal Taliaferro (Baxter), John Merton (Ed Harris), John Hamilton (Walsh), Tom Chatterton (Merchant), Tom Bondon (James Bradley), Jack Kirk (Wetherby), Jay Kirby (Randolph Meredith), Si Jenks (Zeke Haydon), Stanley Price (Hedges), Tom Steele (Ed Hull), Duke Green (Evans), Dale Van Sickel (Danley).

Synopsis: Barbara Meredith (**Linda Stirling**) takes on the identity of the Black Whip, a masked rider who avenges wrong with gun and cattle whip after the death of her father. Working with her to further the newspaper campaign in favor of the Union is a government agent, Vic Gordon (**George J. Lewis**), who does not learn of the Whip's identity until he has been twice saved by her from the outlaw gang. Leading the forces against them is Dan Hammond (**Francis McDonald**), the owner of the city stage line at the head of a band of renegades.

Locations: Iverson Movie Ranch, Republic Studio backlot and Los Angeles River.

The Los Angeles River which cut through the studio property (Chapter 10).

Three views of the Iverson Movie Ranch.

Chapter 7.

Chapter 5.

Chapter 1.

Republic Studio backlot.

Western Street (Chapter 1).

Western Street (Chapter 1).

Western Street—behind the blacksmith building was a building containing cave sets (Chapter 4).

Republic Studio backlot.

Chapter 5.

Chapter 4.

Matte painting on the upper portion of the frame which was shot at the cliffs/caves sets. Chapter 4.

Manhunt of Mystery Island
(1945)

Directors: Spencer Bennet, Wallace A. Grissell, and Yakima Canutt. **Cast:** Richard Bailey (Lance Reardon), Linda Stirling (Claire Forrest), Roy Barcroft (Captain Mephisto), Kenne Duncan (Sidney Brand), Forrest Taylor (William Forrest), Forbes Murray (Henry Hargraves), Jack Ingram (Edward Armstrong), Harry Strang (Fred Braley), Edward Cassidy (Paul Melton), Frank Allen (John Raymond), Lane Chandler (Reed), Russ Vincent (Ruga), Dale Van Sickel (Barker), Tom Steele (Lyons), Duke Green (Spencer Harvey).

Synopsis: A breakthrough scientific device will revolutionize the world's energy usage if the kidnapped creator can be found. To rescue her father, Claire Forrest (**Linda Stirling**) enlists the help of private detective, Lance Reardon (**Richard Bailey**). Clues lead them to a remote Pacific isle known only as Mystery Island, where the two confront sinister and astonishing forces. The descendants of a long-dead pirate, Captain Mephisto (**Roy Barcroft**) are holding the scientist for their own gain. Worst of all, one of the heirs possesses a Transformation Machine with the impossible ability of changing him into the molecular duplicate of his ancestor, Mephisto.

Locations: Iverson Movie Ranch, Dana Point Harbor, Lewis Mansion, Casa Dorinda (stock), Stearns Wharf (stock), Republic Studio backlot.

The Arches at Dana Point (Chapter 1).

Three views of the Iverson Movie Ranch.

One of the last remaining sets at the ranch after construction of housing began. Chapter 13.

The concrete bridge at the Upper Iverson property. Chapter 13.

Chapter 12.

Three views of the Iverson Movie Ranch.

Chapter 12.

Chapter 4.

Chapter 4.

Three images of the George Lewis mansion was designed by architect Albert Farr and was erected on 10 acres of land in Benedict Canyon. Unfortunately, the mansion was eventually torn down.

Chapter 1.

Chapter 2.

Chapter 2.

MANHUNT OF MYSTERY ISLAND

Three views of Dana Point Harbor pier.

Chapter 11.

Chapter 9.

Chapter 9.

Three views of Dana Point Harbor.

Chapter 3.

Chapter 3.

Chapter 9.

MANHUNT OF MYSTERY ISLAND

Republic Studio backlot.

New York Street. Chapter 7.

New York Street. Chapter 7.

New York Street. Chapter 7.

Federal Operator 99
(1945)

Directors: Spencer Bennet, Wallace A. Grissell, and Yakima Canutt. **Cast:** Marten Lamont (Jerry Blake), Helen Talbot (Joyce Kingston), George J. Lewis (Jim Belmont), Lorna Gray (Rita Parker), Hal Taliaferro (Matt Farrell), LeRoy Mason (Morton), Bill Stevens (Fred Martin), Maurice Cass (Giuseppe Morello), Kernan Cripps (Tom Jeffries), Elaine Lange (Countess Delremy), Frank Jaquet (Warren Hunter), Forrest Taylor (Otto Wolfe), Jay Novello (Heinrick), Tom London (Crawford), Jack Ingram (Riggs).

Synopsis: Crime lord James 'Jim' Belmont (**George J. Lewis**) escapes FBI custody and resumes his criminal empire, only to be thwarted at every turning point by British-accented Jerry Blake, the FBI's Operator 99 (**Marten Lamont**). Belmont plots to steal the crown jewels of the Princess Cornelia, with the aid of his cohorts Matt Farrell (**Hal Taliaferro**), Rita Parker (**Lorna Gray**), and his crafty secretary Morton (**LeRoy Mason**). Blake's secretary Joyce Kingston (**Helen Talbot**) gets involved in directly helping Blake thwart Belmont.

Locations: 14601 Aetna Street, Republic Studio front lot and backlot.

Unidentified theater interior (Chapter 12).

Three views of this building on the corner of Aetna Street and Vesper Ave. Address is 14601 Aetna Street. Located in the San Fernando Valley. All three images are from Chapter 9.

Republic Studio backlot New York Street for all three views.

Chapter 1.

Chapter 1.

Chapter 1.

Republic Studio front lot.

Exiting the writer's building (Chapter 1).

Administration building in the background (Chapter 1).

Writer's building (left) and Administration building (right) (Chapter 1).

Republic Studio Main Lot buildings.

Arriving at the door to the Music and Accounting Department at Stage 12 (Chapter 9).

Car is in front of the Men's and Women's Wardrobe building as it turns. The building on the left is the Transportatioin Department (Chapter 9).

Inside one of the working buildings (unidentified) (Chapter 4)

Unidentified Locations:

Chapter 1,

Chapter 1.

Chapter 10.

The Purple Monster Strikes (1945)

Directors: Spencer Bennet and Fred Brannon. **Cast:** Dennis Moore (Craig Foster), Linda Stirling (Sheila Layton), Roy Barcroft (The Purple Monster), James Craven (Cyrus Layton), Bud Geary (Hodge Garrett), Mary Moore (Marcia), John Davidson (Emperor of Mars), Joe Whitehead (Carl Stewart), Emmett Vogan (Saunders), George Carleton (Paul Meredith), Kenne Duncan (Charles Mitchell), Rosemonde James (Helen), Monte Hale (Harvey), Wheaton Chambers (Benjamin), Frederick Howard (Crandall), Anthony Warde (Tony), Ken Terrell (Andy Martin).

Synopsis: Dr. Cyrus Layton (**James Craven**), inventor of an airship capable of flying to other planets, is murdered by the Purple Monster (**Roy Barcroft**). This Monster arrives by rocket from Mars for the sole purpose of stealing his victim's plans and preparing an invasion of Earth by the Martian army. Before his death, Dr. Layton succeeds in summoning Larry Foster (**Dennis Moore**). Larry, with the scientist's young niece, Sheila (**Linda Stirling**), arrive just as the Monster takes on the physical aspects of her father.

Locations: Iverson Ranch, Griffith Park Observatory, Republic Studio front lot and backlot.

Unidentified location (Chapter 3).

Three views of the Iverson Movie Ranch.

Chapter 12.

Chapter 12.

Chapter 1.

Republic Studio backlot.

Brazos Street. Chapter 15.

Road between Western Street and New York Street. Chapter 12.

Chapter 12.

THE PURPLE MONSTER STRIKES 257

Republic Studio front lot.

Outside the walls of the studio (Chapter 9).

Truck at the loading dock for the Property Department (Chapter 3).

Inside a working building (Chapter 1).

The Griffith Park Observatory.

Both images are from Chapter 1.

The Phantom Rider
(1945)

Directors: Spencer Bennet and Fred Brannon. **Cast:** Robert Kent (James Sterling), Peggy Stewart (Doris Shannon), LeRoy Mason (Fred Carson), George J. Lewis (Blue Feather), Kenne Duncan (Ben Brady), Hal Taliaferro (Nugget), Chief Thundercloud (Yellow Wolf), Tom London (Ceta), Roy Barcroft (Marshal), Monte Hale (Cass), John Hamilton (Williams), Hugh Prosser (Keeler), Jack Kirk (Turner), Rex Lease (Randall), Tommy Coats (Tim), Joe Yrigoyen (Blackie), Bill Yrigoyen (Indian Renegade).

Synopsis: Dr. Jim Sterling (**Robert Kent**) attempts to create a police force on the Big Tree Indian Reservation. However, his efforts face sabotage, secretly directed by the apparently friendly Indian Agent Fred Carson (**LeRoy Mason**), whose gang is currently able to rob stagecoaches wagons without opposition. In order to defeat his enemies, Sterling adopts the name and costume of the legendary "Phantom Rider".

Locations: Iverson Movie Ranch, Corriganville, Republic Studio backlot.

Republic Studio backlot cave set (Chapter 4).

Three view of the Corriganville Movie Ranch. All views are from Chapter 1.

The church/school house was located just to the east of Silvertown, the western street at the ranch (only partially built at the time of the filming).

Three views of the Iverson Movie Ranch. All are from Chapter 1.

Three views of the Iverson Movie Ranch.

The Wrench Rock on the Upper Iverson. Chapter 2.

This cabin became the Lone Ranger's silver mine in the television series. Chapter 3.

A temporary set for the serial. Chapter 6.

Republic Studio backlot.

Western Street. Chapter 11.

Western Street. Chapter 7.

Western Street. Chapter 1.

King of the Forest Rangers
(1946)

Directors: Spencer Bennet and Fred Brannon. **Cast:** Larry Thompson (Steve King), Helen Talbot (Marion Brennan), Stuart Hamblen (Carver), Anthony Warde (Burt Spear), LeRoy Mason (Flush Haliday), Scott Elliott (Andrews), Tom London (Tom Judson), Walter Soderling (Miner), Bud Geary (Rance Barton), Harry Strang (Hank), Ernie Adams (Hiram Bailey), Eddie Parker (Stover), Jack Kirk (Holmes), Tom Steele (Martin), Dale Van Sickel (Blaine), Stanley Blystone (Harry Lynch).

Synopsis: Delivering supplies to a Forest Park campsite where Professor Carver (**Stuart Hamblen**) and Martin (**Tom Steele**) are supposedly investigating Antelope Tower. Amateur archeologist Tom Judson (**Tom London**) produces half of a picture rug woven with cryptic animal and arrow symbols and states his theory of buried treasure. He then shows the partial map to Steve King (**Larry Thompson**).

Locations: Big Bear, Republic Studio backlot.

Boulder Bay at Big Bear Lake (Chapter 1).

Three views of Big Bear.
All from Chapter 1.

Republic Studio backlot.

Brazos Street. Chapter 1.

Duchess Ranch barn. Chapter 9.

Duchess Ranch house. Chapter 3.

Daughter of Don Q
(1946)

Directors: Spencer Bennet and Fred Brannon. **Cast:** Adrian Booth (Dolores Quantaro), Kirk Alyn (Cliff Roberts), LeRoy Mason (Carlos Manning), Roy Barcroft (Mel Donovan), Claire Meade (Maria Montenez), Kernan Cripps (Grogan), Jimmy Ames (Romero), Eddie Parker (George Tompkins), Tom Steele (Norton), Dale Van Sickel (Murphy), Fred Graham (Rollins), Tom Quinn (R. J. Riggs), Johnny Daheim (Morris Kelso), Ted Mapes (Ned Gray), Stanford Jolley (Lippy Monroe), Buddy Roosevelt (Moody).

Synopsis: The proprietor of an antique shop discovers an ancient land grant giving Don Quantaro, an early settler of California, a large tract of land which is now the business district of a city and worth millions. One of the descendants of Don Q, Carlos Manning (**LeRoy Mason**) decides he wants the land for himself and so begins to murder all his relatives. One of these relatives, Dolores Quantero (**Lorna Gray**), joins forces with a newspaper reporter, Cliff Roberts (**Kirk Alyn**) and tracks down the fiend.

Locations: Big Tujunga Narrows Bridge, Chatsworth Train Depot (stock), Chatsworth (stock), Republic Studio backlot.

Unidentified location. Chapter 1.

Big Tujunga Narrows Bridge, Angelus Crest Highway. Chapter 12.

Unidentified location. Chapter 4.

Unidentified location. Chapter 1.

Republic Studio backlot.

New York Street (Chapter 1).

New York Street (Chapter 1).

Duchess Ranch (Chapter 10).

Republic Studio backlot cave entrance at their Cliffs and Caves set. Chapter 7.

Republic Studio backlot cave set. Chapter 7.

The Crimson Ghost
(1946)

Directors: William Witney and Fred C. Brannon. **Cast:** Charles Quigley (Duncan Richards), Linda Stirling (Diana Farnsworth), Clayton Moore (Louis Ashe), I. Stanford Jolley (Blackton), Kenne Duncan (Chambers), Forrest Taylor (Van Wyck), Emmett Vogan (Anderson), Sam Flint (Maxwell), Joe Forte (Parker), Stanley Price (Fator), Wheaton Chambers (Wilson), Tom Steele (Stricker), Dale Van Sickel (Harte), Rex Lease (Bain), Fred Graham (Zane), Bud Wolfe (Cross).

Synopsis: The masked Crimson Ghost (**Joseph Forte**) is determined to steal the Cyclotrode X, a device designed to repel atomic bomb attacks and that can disable electrical devices. Its inventor, university professor Dr. Chambers (**Kenne Duncan**), demonstrates its powers at a faculty meeting by having it detect and fell a model airplane. After the meeting, two of the Ghost's henchmen attempt to steal the device, but Chambers destroys it to prevent them from doing so. Criminologist Duncan Richards (**Charles Quigley**), a colleague of Chambers, arrives and fights the henchmen. One of them, Ashe (**Clayton Moore**), escapes, and the other is killed when a collar around his neck is removed.

Locations: Iverson Movie Ranch, Canoga Park High School, Chatsworth Inn, Stearns Wharf (stock).

The Chatsworth Inn was built in 1890. For most of its life, it stood at 9820 Topanga Canyon Blvd. in Chatsworth. Chapter 3.

Canoga Park High School.

Chapter 1.

Chapter 4.

Chapter 12.

THE CRIMSON GHOST

Iverson Movie Ranch.

Strolling along an Upper Iverson roadway. Chapter 2.

Overlooking the San Fernando Valley from the Lower Iverson. Chapter 6.

Lower Iverson. Chapter 4.

Iverson Movie Ranch.

The top of Nyoka Cliff. Chapter 6.

Chapter 10.

Main chase road on the Upper Iverson. Chapter 10.

The Son of Zorro
(1947)

Directors: Spencer Bennet and Fred C. Brannon. **Cast:** George Turner (Jeffrey Stewart), Peggy Stewart (Kate Wells), Roy Barcroft (Boyd), Edward Cassidy (Moody), Ernie Adams (Hyde), Stanley Price (Pancho), Edmund Cobb (Stockton), Ken Terrell (George Thomas), Wheaton Chambers (Caleb Baldwin), Fred Graham (Quirt), Eddie Parker (Melton), Si Jenks (Fred), Jack O'Shea (Hood), Jack Kirk (Charlie Grimes), Tom Steele (Leach), Dale Van Sickle (Murray).

Synopsis: Jeff Stewart (**George Turner**), a cavalry officer, returns to his home in the West at the close of the Civil War to find a ring of crooks operating in the important offices of the county government. To fight these men, Jeff puts on a black mask, jumps on his horse, and, as Zorro, rides to the rescue.

Locations: Iverson Movie Ranch, Republic Studio backlot and Los Angeles River.

A portion of the Los Angeles River which ran through the Republic Studio property. Chapter 1.

Upper Iverson Movie Ranch.

Chapter 7.

Chapter 1.

Chapter 8.

Republic Studio backlot.

Western Street. Chapter 1.

Western Street. Chapter 6.

Western Street. Chapter 1.

Republic Studio backlot.

Duchess Ranch . Chapter 2.

Melody Ranch early building. Chapter 1.

Back side of the Duchess Ranch. Chapter 1.

Jesse James Rides Again
(1947)

Directors: Fred C. Brannon and Thomas Carr. **Cast:** Clayton Moore (Jesse James), Linda Stirling (Ann Bolton), Roy Barcroft (Frank Lawton), John Compton (Steve Lane), Tristram Coffin (James Clark), Tom London (Sam Bolton), Holly Bane (Tim), Edmund Cobb (Wilkie), Gene Stutenroth (Duffie), Fred Graham (Amos Hawks), LeRoy Mason (Finlay), Edward Cassidy (Grant), Dave Anderson (Sam), Eddie Parker (Flint), Tom Steele (Goff), Dale Van Sickel (Brock).

Synopsis: Gunfighter Jesse James (**Clayton Moore**) is framed for a Missouri bank job and murder by a black-cowled outlaw gang, known as "The Black Raiders". Unable to clear his name, he and companion Steve Lane (**John Compton**), whose father was murdered during the bank robbery, flee to escape the posse. They ride into a town where they receive shelter from Ann Bolton (**Linda Stirling**) and her elderly father, Sam Bolton (**Tom London**), whose ranch is being regularly attacked by The Black Raiders. The same gang are led by Frank Lawton (**Roy Barcroft**), who in turn had been hired by James Clark (**Tristram Coffin**), a businessman. Through him, The Black Raiders attempt to drive the Boltons and other farmers off their land because of localized oil reserves in the area.

Locations: Iverson Movie Ranch, Republic Studio backlot.

Miniature Pool. Chapter 1.

Upper Iverson Movie Ranch.

Chapter 1.

Chapter 3.

Chapter 3.

Republic Studio backlot.

Western Street . Chapter 1.

Duchess Ranch. Chapter 1.

Western Street. Chapter 1.

Republic Studio backlot.

Melody Ranch. Chapter 2.

The Lagoon. Chapter 1.

Dakota Street. Chapter 4.

The Black Widow
(1947)

Directors: Spencer Bennet and Fred C. Brannon. **Cast:** Bruce Edwards (Steven Colt), Virginia Lindley (Joyce Winters), Carol Forman (Sombra), Anthony Warde (Nick Ward), Ramsay Ames (Ruth Dayton), I. Stanford Jolley (Z. V. Jaffa), Theodore Gottlieb (Hitomu), Virginia Carroll (Ann Curry), Gene Stutenroth (John M. Walker), Sam Flint (Henry Weston), Tom Steele (Bard), Dale Van Sickel (Bill), LeRoy Mason (Godfrey), Forrest Taylor (Bradley), Ernie Adams (Blinky), Keith Richards (Michael Burns).

Synopsis: The Editor of the *Daily Clarion* newspaper, John M. Walker (**Gene Stutenroth**) hires amateur criminologist Steve Colt (**Bruce Edwards**) to solve a series of murders, all involving venomous spider bites. Meanwhile, King Hitomu (**Theodore Gottlieb**) has sent his daughter Sombra (**Carol Forman**) to the United States to fulfill his plan for global domination. There she poses as a fortune teller and, with a gang of henchmen, attempts to steal a prototype Atomic Rocket Engine using her uncanny ability to impersonate other women.

Locations: Iverson Movie Ranch, Santa Susanna Pass Road, Topanga Canyon Road (probably stock), 13271 Moorpark Street (stock), Republic Studio backlot.

Barracks National Home for Disabled Volunteer Soldiers. Chapter 9.

Topanga Canyon Road, just south of Stony Point, Chatsworth. Chapter 5.

Turning west onto Chatsworth Street from Topanga Canyon Road, Chatsworth. Chapter 5.

Chatsworth Street, just west of Topanga Canyon Road, Chatsworth. Chapter 5.

The route 66 sign is a fake as that road never came close to Chatsworth.

THE BLACK WIDOW

Iverson Movie Ranch.

Chapter 8.

Chapter 5.

Western Street. Chapter 3.

Republic Studio backlot.

New York Street. Chapter 1.

New York Street. Chapter 1.

New York Street. Chapter 1.

Republic Studio backlot.

New York Square. Chapter 8.

New York Square. Chapter 13.

New York Street. Chapter 13.

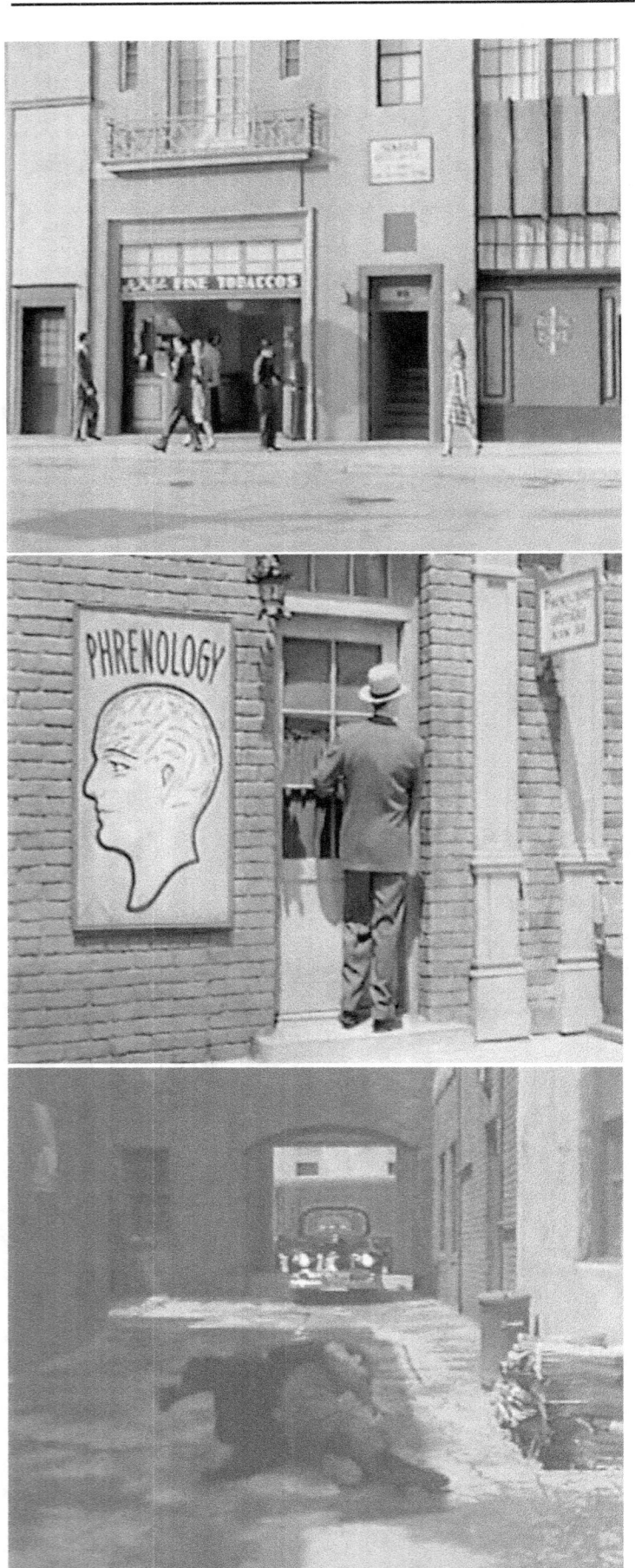

Republic Studio backlot.

New York Square. Chapter 7.

New York Street. Chapter 7.

Alley between Western Street and New York Square. Chapter 7.

Republic Studio front lot.

The Mill Building. Chapter 8.

Loading dock to the Property Department. Chapter 4.

Republic Studio backlot. New York Street. Chapter 8.

G-Men Never Forget
(1948)

Directors: Fred Brannon and Yakima Canutt. **Cast:** Clayton Moore (Ted O'Hara), Roy Barcroft (Angus Cameron), Ramsay Ames (Frances Blake), Drew Allen (Duke Graham), Tom Steele (Parker), Dale Van Sickel (Fred Brent), Edmund Cobb (R. J. Cook), Stanley Price (Robert Benson), Jack O'Shea (Slater), Barry Brooks (George), Doug Aylesworth (Hayden), Frank O'Connor (McLain), Dian Fauntelle (Miss Stewart), Eddie Acuff (Fiddler), George Magrill (Staley), Ken Terrell (John Kelsey).

Synopsis: Escaped criminal Victor Murkland (**Roy Barcroft**) kidnaps the police commissioner and, with the aid of plastic surgery, takes his place. Federal Agent Ted O'Hara (**Clayton Moore**) is called in to try to stop the wave of crime initiated by Murkland, not knowing that Murkland is posing as the police commissioner and is aware of O'Haras' every move. The real commissioner is being held captive in a mental hospital run by Dr. Benson (**Stanley Price**). O'Hara is aided by the beautiful Sgt. Frances Blake (**Ramsay Ames**). Murkland's gang threatens to destroy a major tunnel being built underneath a channel, and blackmails the builder into paying him protection money.

Locations: Iverson Movie Ranch, Studio City, Republic Studio front lot and backlot.

An empty lot on the Ventura Blvd. side of the studio with only the alley between their fence and the lot. Double as "Fiddler's Best Cars". (Chapter 3).

Three views of the Iverson Movie Ranch.

Chapter 6.

Chapter 1.

Chapter 1.

The streets of Stansbury Avenue and Valley Vista Blvd. All three images are from Chapter 2.

Republic Studio Backlot.

New York Street. Chapter 1.

Wyoming Set. Located west of the Duchess Ranch. The Mansion set would replace it the following year. Chapter 1.

Alley between Western Street and New York Square. Chapter 11.

Dangers of the Canadian Mounted (1948)

Directors: Fred Brannon and Yakima Canutt. **Cast:** Jim Bannon (Christopher Royal), Virginia Belmont (Roberta Page), Anthony Warde (Mort Fowler), Dorothy Granger (Skagway Kate), Bill Van Sickel (Dan Page), Tom Steele (Fagin), Dale Van Sickel (Boyd), I. Stanford Jolley (J. P. Belanco), Phil Warren (George Hale), Lee Morgan (Dale), James Dale (Andrew Knight), Ted Adams (Meggs), JOhn Crawford (Danton), Jack Clifford (Marshal), Eddy Parker (Lowry), Frank O'Connor (Barton).

Synopsis: A criminal gang discovers a Genghis Khan treasure ship on the Canada-Alaska border. However, the treasure itself is hidden on land. In their efforts to find the hidden riches, they resort to murder and sabotage to stop the construction of the Alcan highway which will bring homesteaders to the area. Sergeant Christopher 'Chris' Royal (**Jim Bannon**) of the Royal Canadian Mounted Police and his allies battle their way to find the crooks, and to learn the identity of their mysterious leader known only as 'The Boss'.

Locations: Big Bear, Republic Studio backlot and Los Angeles River.

The temporary fort gateway which was erected for *Northwest Outpost*. You can seen the Melody Ranch barn inside, and to the right and back of this shot is the Brazos Street. Chapter 7.

DANGERS OF THE CANADIAN MOUNTED

Three views of Big Bear.

Chapter 1.

Chapter 2.

Chapter 8.

Republic Studio backlot.

Brazos Street. Chapter 1.

Brazos Street. Chapter 1.

Duchess Ranch. Chapter 1.

Republic Studio Backlot.

The canyon between the Cliffs. Chapter 1..

A shipwreck in front of the Cliffs.. Chapter 1.

Western Street. Chapter 3.

Three views of the Big Bear Airport from Chapter 4.

Adventures of Frank and Jesse James (1948)

Directors: Fred Brannon and Yakima Canutt. **Cast:** Clayton Moore (Jesse James), Steve Darrell (Frank James), Noel Neill (Judy Powell), George J. Lewis (Rafe Henley), Stanley Andrews (Jim Powell), John Crawford (Amos Ramsey), Sam Flint (Paul Thatcher), House Peters, Jr. (Towey), Dale Van Sickel (Thomas Dale), Tom Steele (Mike Steele), James Dale (J. B. Nichols), I. Stanford Jolley (Ward), Gene Stutenroth (Marshal), Lane Bradford (Bill), George Chesebro (Jim), Jack Kirk (Casey).

Synopsis: The notorious James brothers, Jesse (**Clayton Moore**) and Frank (**Steve Darrell**) jointly own a supposedly played-out silver mine, which they plan to reopen to get money to make restitution to victims of their gang's robberies. Banker Paul Thatcher (**Sam Flint**) lends them money, but puts in Amos Ramsey (**John Crawford**) as manager. When gold is found, Ramsey kills Jim Powell (**Stanley Andrews**), conceals the discovery, and hires Rafe Henley (**George J. Lewis**) and his outlaw band, who do his bidding by keeping the mine from operating, preventing its value being discovered.

Locations: Iverson Movie Ranch, Republic Studio backlot.

Republic Studios backlot, Dakota Street. Chapter 10.

Three view of the Iverson Movie Ranch.

Chapter 2.

Chapter 2.

Chapter 3.

Republic Studio backlot.

Western Street. Chapter 2.

Western Street. Chapter 4.

Duchess Ranch. Chapter 1.

Federal Agents vs. Underworld, Inc. (1949)

Director: Fred C. Brannon. **Cast:** Kirk Alyn (David Worth), Rosemary LaPlanche (Laura Keith), Roy Barcroft (Spade Gordon), Carol Forman (Nila), James Dale (Steve Eans), Bruce Edwards (Paul Williams), James Craven (James Clayton), Tristram Coffin (Frank Chambers), Tom Steele (Tim Grey), Dale Van Sickel (Mac), Jack O'Shea (Ali), Marshall Reed (O'Hara), Bob Wilke (Zod), Robert St. Angelo (Native 3), Dave Anderson (Porter).

Synopsis: Nila (**Carol Forman**), an Abistahnian criminal, and Spade Gordon (**Roy Barcroft**), an American gangster, conspire to form a super-mob dubbed Underworld, Incorporated, funded by the treasure of Kurigal I of Abistahn, instructions for the location of which are contained in hieroglyphics written on two golden statues in the shape of hands, found in Kurigal's tomb. When the professor in charge of the tomb's dig disappears under mysterious circumstances while translating the writing on one of the hands back at his American office, a team of special government agents led by David Worth (**Kirk Alyn**) and his aide Steve Evans, assisted by the professor's aide Laura Keith (**Rosemary La Planche**), set out to find the professor and the now-missing hands. The criminals manage to get possession of one of the Hands, but they need both of them to recreate the treasure map.

Locations: Chatsworth Depot, Chatsworth, Republic Studio front lot and backlot.

Probably stock footage of Sunset Blvd. The Chateau Marmont is on the left at 8232 Sunset Blvd, and the Granville Towers (White Building). Eisode 1.

Chatsworth Train Depot.
Chapter 9.

Chatsworth Hardware Store, 21920 Devonshire Street.
Chapter 7.

Crisler Building, southeast corner of Devonshire Street and Topanga Canyon Blvd., Chatsworth.
Chapter 7.

Iverson Movie Ranch.

Chapter 11.

Iverson Movie Ranch.
Chapter 11.

Arboretum (stock footage).
Chapter 5.
In January 1947, the State of California and County of Los Angeles purchased 111 acres at the center of the Rancho Santa Anita for $320,000. Named the Los Angeles County Arboretum & Botanic Garden, it is located at 301N S Baldwin Ave, Arcadia.

Republic Studios Front Lot.

The Writers Building.
Chapter 5.

The loading dock to the Property Department (building behind car is where the transformers were housed. Chapter 4.

The Cooling Factory near the Mansion set behind Stage 10.
Chapter 5.

Ghost of Zorro
(1949)

Director: Fred C. Brannon. **Cast:** Clayton Moore (Ken Mason), Pamela Blake (Rita White), Roy Barcroft (Hank Kilgore), George J. Lewis (Moccasin), Eugene Roth (George Crane), John Crawford (Mulvaney), I. Standford Jolley (Paul Hobson), Steve Clark (Jonathan R. White), Steve Darrell (Ben Simpson), Dale Van Sickel (Mike Hodge), Tom Steele (Brace), Alex Montoya (Yellow Hawk), Marshall Reed (Fowler), Frank O'Connor (Doctor), Jack O'Shea (Freight Agent), Holly Bane (Larkin).

Synopsis: Ken Mason/Zorro (Clayton Moore), eastern surveyor, is employed by Jonathan R. White (**Steve Clark**) and his daughter, Rita White (**Pamela Blake**), operators of a telegraph company, to lead their operations in extending their lines. Jonathan R. White is killed in an Indian attack instigated by George Crane (**Eugene Roth**), who opposes the telegraph company because its completion would tend to destroy his private empire.

Locations: Iverson Movie Ranch, Corriganville (stock), Lone Pine (stock), Republic Studio backlot.

A publicity photo showing the Republic Studio backlot cave set.

GHOST OF ZORRO

Iverson Movie Ranch.
Chapter 1.

Above: A publicity shot taken on top of the lookout point behind the Garden of the Gods and across from the Nyoka Cliff, at the Lower Iverson Movie Rach.

Republic Studios Back Lot

Western Street. Chapter 1.

Western Street. Chapter 1.

Western Street. Chapter 1.

King of the Rocket Men
(1949)

Director: Fred C. Brannon. **Cast:** Tristram Coffin (Jeffrey King), Mae Clarke (Glenda Thomas), Don Haggerty (Tony Dirken), House Peters Jr. (Burt Winslow), James Craven (Millard), I. Stanford Jolley (Bryant), Douglas Evans (Chairman), Ted Adams (Martin Conway), Stanley Price (Gunther Von Strum), Dale Van Sickel (Martin), Tom Steele (Knox), David Sharpe (Blears), Eddie Parker (Rowan), Michael Ferro (Turk), Frank O'Connor (Guard), Buddy Roosevelt (Phillips).

Synopsis: An evil genius of unknown identity, calling himself "Dr. Vulcan" (**I. Stanford Jolley**) (heard only as a voice and seen as a mysterious shadow on a brightly lit wall), plots to conquer the world. He needs to first eliminate, one by one, the members of the Science Associates, an organization of America's greatest scientists. After narrowly escaping an attempt on his life by Vulcan, one member of Science Associates, Dr. Millard (**James Craven**) goes into hiding. He soon outfits another member, Jeff King (**Tristram Coffin**) with an advanced, atomic-powered rocket backpack, attached to a leather jacket with a bullet-shaped, aerodynamic flight helmet, and a raygun that they had been developing together. Using the flying jacket and helmet and other inventions provided by Dr. Millard, and aided by magazine reporter and photographer Glenda Thomas (**Mae Clarke**), Jeff King, as Rocket Man, battles Vulcan and his henchmen.

Locations: Iverson Movie Ranch, Sunset Tower Hotel, Occidental College (stock), Conejo Valley Airport (stock), Republic Studio backlot and front lot.

Republic front lot. Rocketman flying over the Mill Building heading towards Stage 4. A glimpse of an edge of a set at New York Square on the left. Chapter 6.

Iverson Movie Ranch.

Chapter 6.

Chapter 1.

Chapter 4.

KING OF THE ROCKET MEN

Republic Studio Front Lot.

Chapter 1.

Chapter 1.

Dressing Rooms on the Side of Stage 3.
Chapter 1.

Republic Studio backlot.

New York Street.
Chapter 1.

New York Street.
Chapter 2.

New York Square.
Chapter 2.

KING OF THE ROCKET MEN

Republic Studios Backlot. Where the man is standing, if you head to the far back, turn right and travel a very short distance, you will find yourself at the closed end of the alley.

Chapter 2.

Front Lot. The Writer's Building. Chapter 4.

New York Street. Chapter 6.

The James Brothers of Missouri (1949)

Director: Fred C. Brannon. **Cast:** Keith Richards (Jesse James), Robert Bice (Frank James), Noel Neill (Peg Royer), Roy Barcroft (Ace Marlin), Patricia Knox (Belle Calhoun), Lane Bradford (Monk Tucker), Eugene Roth (Rand), John Hamilton (Lon Royer), Edmund Cobb (Sheriff), Hank Patterson (Duffy), Dale Van Sickel (Harry Sharkey), Tom Steele (Slim), Lee Roberts (Brandy Jones), Frank O'Connor (Citizen), Marshall Reed (Dutch), Wade Ray (Deputy), Nolan Leary (Pop Keever).

Synopsis: Jesse James (**Keith Richards**) and Frank James (Robert Bice) go undercover to help a former member of their gang, who is now running a respectable freight business but is is being attacked by a rival, Ace Marlin (**Roy Barcroft**) who is trying to drive him out of business. When their former colleague is murdered, the brothers stick around to help his daughter, Peg Royer (**Noel Neill**), who is now in charge of the business, and stop the attacks.

Locations: Iverson Movie Ranch, Corriganville (stock), Burro Flats (stock), Republic Studio backlot.

Unidentified location, probably a stock shot. Chapter 10.

Iverson Movie Ranch. Chapter 1.

Chapter 1.

Atop the overlook behind the Garden of the Gods—Nyoka Cliff in this background. Chapter 3.

Iverson Movie Ranch

Upper Iverson Fake Cave Entrance next to the Lone Ranger cabin.
Chapter 6.

Lone Ranger cabin on the upper Iverson Ranch.
Chapter 7.

Lower Iverson Ranch cabin.
Chapter 7.

Republic Studios Back Lot

Western Street. Chapter 1.

Western Street. Chapter 1.

Western Street. Chapter 7.

Republic Studios Back Lot

Duchess Ranch. Chapter 5.

Spanish Street. Chapter 2.

Backlot cave set. Chapter 2.

Radar Patrol vs. Spy King
(1949)

Director: Fred C. Brannon. **Cast:** Kirk Alyn (Chris Calvert), Jean Dean (Joan Hughes), Anthony Warde (Ricco Morgan), George J. Lewis (Manuel Agura), Eve Whitney (Nitra), John Merton (John Baroda), Tristram Coffin (Franklyn Lord), John Crawford (Sands), Harold Goodwin (Miller), Dale Van Sickel (Lentz), Tom Steele (Gorman), Eddie Parker (Dutch), Forbes Murray (Committeeman 2), Frank O'Connor (Committeeman 1), Stephen Gregory (Hugo), Frank Dae (John Clark), Arvon Dale (Trooper).

Synopsis: John Baroda (**John Merton**), a neo-Nazi and his alter ego, *The Spy King* and his aide Nitra (**Eve Whitney**), are part of a sabotaging team for a vast defense system of radar stations along the U. S. borders. Radar Defense Bureau operative Chris Calvert (**Kirk Alyn**) comes to the rescue of radar scientist, Joan Hughes (**Jean Dean**), who has been kidnapped by Baroda's henchmen.

Locations: Iverson Movie Ranch, Chatsworth (stock), Sheldon Street, Republic Studio backlot and front lot.

The Stonehurst Market, 11148 Sheldon Street. Chapter 2.

Iverson Movie Ranch.

Chapter 5.

Chapter 8.

Chapter 9.

Unidentified location. Chapter 5.

Sheldon Street and Wealtha Ave. The stone pillar is still there. Chapter 2.

Unidentified location. Chapter 7

Republic Studio backlot.

Western Street.
Chapter 1.

Western Street.
Chapter 2.

Western Street.
Chapter 6.

Republic Studio Front Lot.

Transportation Department.
Chapter 2.

Property Department Loading Dock..
Chapter 3.

Nearing the loading dock of the
Property Department.
Chapter 3.

The Invisible Monster (1950)

Director: Fred C. Brannon. **Cast:** Richard Webb (Lane Carson), Aline Towne (Carol Richards), Lane Bradford (Burton), Stanley Price (The Phantom Ruler), John Crawford (Harris), George Meeker (Harry Long), Keith Richards (Doctor), Dale Van Sickel (Otto Wagner), Tom Steele (Bill Haines), Marshall Reed (MacDuff), Forrest Burns (Joe), Ed Parker (Stoner), Frank O'Connor (Hogan), Chas. Regan (Art), Charles Sullivan (Grogarty), Howard Mitchell (Watchman 4), Bud Wolfe (Harding).

Synopsis: The Phantom Ruler (**Stanley Price**), also known as the "invisible monster", heads a crime ring mainly due to his ability by chemically treated clothing and light rays to make himself invisible. His slaves are intelligent, smuggled-in aliens afraid he will expose them to government authorities. After a bank vault robbery, Lane Carson (**Richard Webb**), insurance company investigator, and his assistant, Carol Richards (**Aline Towne**), trail one of the aliens who helped The Phantom Ruler with the theft, but the "monster" kills him before they can make him talk.

Locations: Iverson Movie Ranch, Valley Village, William K. English Blacksmith Shop, Republic Studio backlot.

13271 Moorpark Street (stock). Chapter 1.

THE INVISIBLE MONSTER

Iverson Movie Ranch.

Chapter 6.

Chapter 7.

Chapter 9.

Iverson Movie Ranch

Chapter 9.

Chapter 9.

Santa Susanna Pass Road.
Chapter 3.

1805 Vine Street. Chapter 1.

1805 Vine Street. Chapter 1.

Reseda Blvd. and Parthenian Street, Northridge.. Chapter 5.

12640 Chandler Blvd (now 5352 Teasdale Avenue), Valley Village.

Arriving at the address.
Chapter 1.

View of the house from the street.
Chapter 1.

Preparing to enter the house.
Chapter 1.

THE INVISIBLE MONSTER

Republic Studios Back Lot

New York Street. Chapter 5.

Cave entrance at the Cliffs. Chapter 6.

Duchess Ranch. Chapter 9.

Desperadoes of the West
(1950)

Director: Fred C. Brannon. **Cast:** Richard Powers (Ward Gordon), Judy Clark (Sally Arnold), Roy Barcroft (Hacker), I. Stanford Jolley (J. B. Dawson), Lee Phelps (Rusty Steele), Lee Roberts (Larson), Cliff Clark (Arnold), Edmund Cobb (Bowers), Hank Patterson (Hardrock Haggerty), Dale Van Sickel (Reed), Tom Steele (Gregg), Sandy Sanders (Kernj), John Cason (Casey), Guy Teague (Jack), Bud Osborne (Joe), Stanley Blystone (Storekeeper).

Synopsis: Ward Gordon (**Richard Powers**) and Colonel Arnold (**Cliff Clark**) head an oil project being worked on a co-op basis by ranchers. Progress is halted by attacks from a group of bandits headed by J. B. "Dude" Dawson (**I. Stanford Jolley**), eastern promoter, who can obtain the property for his eastern company if he can prevent the others from striking oil.

Locations: Iverson Movie Ranch, Republic Studio backlot.

Unidentified oil drilling location. Chapter 8.

DESPERADOES OF THE WEST

Iverson Movie Ranch.

Chapter 2.

Chapter 5.

Chapter 12.

Republic Studios Back Lot

Western Street. Chapter 1.

Western Street. Chapter 1.

Duchess Ranch. Chapter 1.

Republic Studios Back Lot.

Dakota Street.
Chapter 3.

Duchess Ranch.
Chapter 6.

Duchess Ranch.
Chapter 8.

Flying Disc Man From Mars
(1950)

Director: Fred C. Brannon. **Cast:** Walter Reed (Kent Fowler), Lois Collier (Helen Hall), Gregory Gay (Mota), James Craven (Bryant), Harry Lauter (Drake), Richard Irving (Ryan), Sandy Sanders (Steve), Michael Carr (Trent), Dale Van Sickel (Watchman), Tom Steele (Taylor), George Sherwood (Gate Guard), Jimmy O'Gatty (Grady), John DeSimone (Curtis), Lester Dorr (Crane), Dick Cogan (Kirk).

Synopsis: Mota (**Gregory Gay**), scientist from Mars, arrives in his strange aircraft, and is shot down by scientist Dr. Bryant (**James Craven**) and Kent Fowler (**Walter Reed**), operator of a private air patrol. Bryant keeps Mota's arrival a secret, and discusses atomic development with him. Bryant learns that Mars is centuries ahead of earth in this respect. Bryant promises Mota to help him organize a force to take over the world, and make it a satellite of Mars, in return for Mota's help in building atomic powered planes and bombs.

Locations: Iverson Movie Ranch, Republic Studio front lot and backlot.

Topanga Canyon Blvd. just south of Liggett Street. Chapter 2.

FLYING DISC MAN FROM MARS

Iverson Movie Ranch.

Three publicity shots taken at the movie ranch.

Iverson Movie Ranch.

Chapter 1.

Chapter 3.

Chapter 8.

Iverson Movie Ranch.

Chapter 5.

Chapter 5.

Chapter 5.

Unidentified location from Chapter 1.

Unidentified location from Chapter 1.

Publicity shot of the location.

Republic Studios Front Lot.

The Property Department loading platform. Chapter 4.

A stock shot showing the same building (on right—stage 4 is the large building) minus the building on its right side. Chapter 3.

The Property Department loading ramp and platform from a different perspective. Chapter 4.

Republic Studios Back Lot.

New York Square.
Chapter 4.

Heading to the alley.
Chapter 4.

In the alley.
Chapter 4.

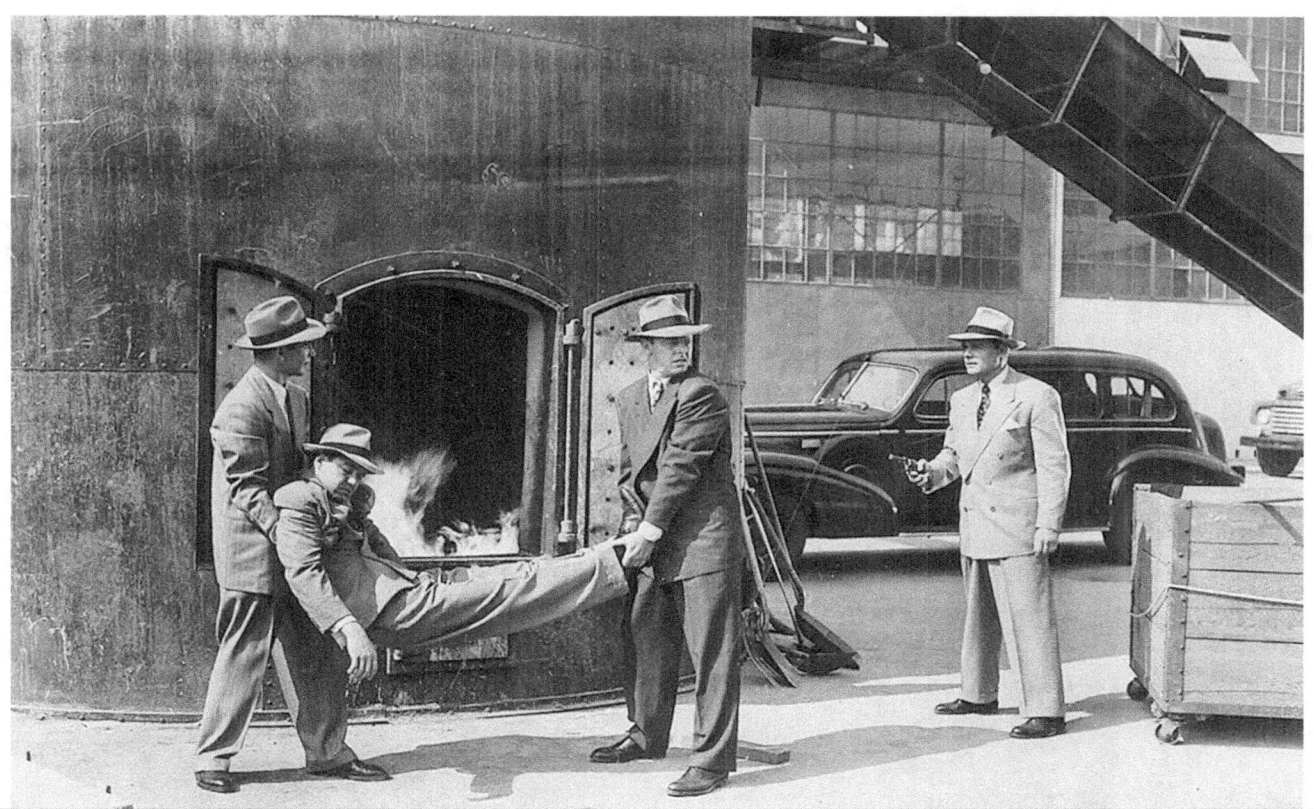

Publicity Shots from Chapter 4
The Incinerator, which was located just north of the Mill Building and south of the backside of the New York Street sets.

Don Daredevil Rides Again
(1951)

Director: Fred C. Brannon. **Cast:** Ken Curtis (Lee Hadley), Aline Towne (Patricia Doyle), Roy Barcroft (Douglas Stratton), Lane Bradford (Weber), Robert Einer (Gary Taylor), John Cason (Hagen), I. Stanford Jolley (Sheriff), Hank Patterson (Buck Bender), Lee Phelps (Michael Doyle), Sandy Sanders (Dirk), Guy Teague (Deputy 1), Tom Steele (Black), Michael Ragan (Miller), Cactus Mack (Turner).

Synopsis: Douglas Stratton (**Roy Barcroft**), crooked attorney and political boss, learns an old Spanish land grant is a forgery, and brings legal action so that all property in the valley reverts to public domain. He has his henchmen attempt to stake out mineral claims and homesteads. Lee Hadley/Don Daredevil (**Ken Curtis**) arrives to protect the property of his cousin, Patricia Doyle (**Aline Towne**), granddaughter of the original owner, and her friends.

Locations: Iverson Movie Ranch, Republic Studio backlot.

Republic Studio Back Lot.

Duchess Ranch Barn interior. Chapter 3.

Iverson Movie Ranch.

Chapter 1.

The lookout behind the Garden of the Gods.
Chapter 2.

The lookout facing towards the Nyoka Cliff.
Chapter 2.

Republic Studios Back Lot.

Duchess Ranch. Chapter 1.

Melody Ranch. Chapter 1.

Dakota Street. Chapter 7.

Republic Studios Back Lot.

Melody Ranch.
Chapter 9.

Dakota Street.
Chapter 5.

Dakota Street.
Chapter 1.

Government Agents vs. Phantom Legion (1951)

Director: Fred C. Brannon. **Cast:** Walter Reed (Hal Duncan), Mary Ellen Kay (Kay Roberts), Dick Curtis (Regan), John Pickard (Sam Bradley), Fred Coby (Cady), Pierce Lyden (Armstrong), George Meeker (Willard), John Phillips (J. J. Patterson), Mauritz Hugo (Thompson), Edmund Cobb (Turner), Eddie Dew (Barnett), George Lloyd (Coroner), Dale Van Sickel (Brice), Tom Steele (Brandt), Arthur Space (Crandall), Norval Mitchell (District Attorney), Frank Meredith (Motorcycle Officer).

Synopsis: Two American government agents, Hal Duncan (**Walter Reed**) and Sam Bradley (**John Pickard**), must prevent agents of a foreign power, led by Regan (**Dick Curtis**) and Cady (**Fred Coby**), from hijacking trucks and stealing defense materials being transported by truck. They are hired by an interstate trucking association whose constituent truck lines have been principal targets of the hijacking, and it becomes evident that one of the four directors of the association is "the Voice," (**Mauritz Hugo**) the secret leader of the gang who provides them with shipment and route information necessary for the gang's success.

Locations: Iverson Movie Ranch, Chatsworth, Sherwood Forest Area, Lake Eleanor, Republic Studio backlot.

Wrights Market, 8753 Reseda Blvd., **Northridge**. Chapter 5.

GOVERNMENT AGENTS VS. PHANTOM LEGION

Southern Pacific Train Tracks at the San Jose Street crossing, Chatsworth..

Arriving at the location.
Chapter 4.

Heading off to plant the bomb.
Chapter 4.

Planting the bomb.
Chapter 4.

Gas Station, northwest corner of Ventura Blvd. and Fallbrook Avenue, Woodland Hills. Chapter 7.

Ventura Blvd. west of Fallbrook Avenue, Woodland Hills. Chapter 10.

Ventura Blvd. west of Fallbrook Avenue, Woodland Hills. Chapter 8.

Northridge Cafe, 8763 Reseda Blvd., Northridge. Chapter 8 and 10.

Wright's Market, 8753 Reseda Blvd., Northridge. Chapter 5.

C and C Market, 8769 Reseda Blvd., Northridge. Chapter 8.

Chatsworth Train Depot.

All three images are from Chapter 2.

Lake Eleanor and Highway 23.

Chapter 3.

Chapter 1.

Chapter 3.

Lake Sherwood Area.

Chapter 1.

Chapter 1.

Chapter 3.

Iverson Movie Ranch.

Overlooking the San Fernando Valley. Chapter 11.

Chapter 4.

Chapter 4.

Republic Studios Front Lot.

Outside the Casting Department.
Chapter 1.

Entering the Transportation Department.
Chapter 7.

Exterior of Stage 3.
Chapter 7.

Republic Studios Back Lot.

New York Street. The Mill Building is in the background. Chapter 5.

Miniature Pool Sea Side Sets. Chapter 5.

Duchess Ranch. Chapter 1.

Radar Men From the Moon (1952)

Director: Fred C. Brannon. **Cast:** George Wallace (Commando Cody), Aline Towne (Joan Gilbert), Roy Barcroft (Retik), William Bakewell (Ted Richards), Clayton Moore (Graber), Peter Brocco (Krog), Bob Stevenson (Daly), Don Walters (Henderson), Tom Steele (Zerg), Dale Van Sickel (Alon), Wilson Wood (Hank), Noel Cravat (Robal), Baynes Barron (Nasor), Paul McGuire (Bream), Ted Thorpe (Bartender), Dick Cogan (Jones).

Synopsis: "Commando Cody" (**George Wallace**), "Sky Marshal of the Universe", works with scientists Joan Gilbert (**Aline Towne**) and Ted Richards (**William Bakewell**) in the development of a flying suit and rocket to the moon. When the nation's defenses are being sabotaged, Wallace learns that an atomic gun is being used by the culprits, and that men on the moon must be responsible.

Locations: Iverson Movie Ranch, Red Rock Canyon, Van Nuys, Los Angeles, Laurel Canyon Bridge, Republic Studio front lot and backlot.

14350 Bessemer Street, Van Nuys. Chapter 5.

RADAR MEN FROM THE MOON

Red Rock Canyon.

Probably the Heliopolis area.
Chapter 1.

Chapter 1.

Chapter 1.

Red Rock Canyon.

Hagen Canyon.

Chapter 3.

Chapter 3.

Chapter 2.

Traveling on South Los Angeles Street.

1929 South Los Angeles Street. Chapter 11.

Olympic Building, 1031 South Los Angeles Street. Chapter 11.

1929 South Los Angeles Street. Chapter 11.

14350 Bessemer Street, Van Nuys.
Chapter 5.

122 East Washington Blvd.
Chapter 11.

Adams Campbell, 1733 South Los Angeles Street.
Chapter 11.

Aetna Street and Sylmar Avenue, Van Nuys. Chapter 5.

Aetna Street and Sylmar Avenue, Van Nuys. Chapter 5.

Turning onto Aetna Street. Velvatone Stucco Co., 14349 Aetna Street.

Laurel Canyon Bridge over the Los Angeles River.

Chapter 3.

Traveiling west on Valleyheart Drive on the south side of the Los Angeles River. The Laurel Canyon Bridge is in the background. Chapter 3.

On Laurel Canyon Blvd., crossing the bridge, headed north.
Chapter 3.

RADAR MEN FROM THE MOON

Lake Sherwood Area.

Chapter 1.

Chapter 1.

Chapter 1.

Iverson Movie Ranch.

Chapter 6.

Chapter 6.

Chapter 6.

Republic Studios Front Lot.

The Writer's Building.
Chapter 1.

New York Square.
Chapter 4.

New York Street.
Chapter 4.

Republic Studios Back Lot.

New York Street.
Chapter 4.

New York Street.
Chapter 4.

Transportation Building on the Front Lot.
Chapter 7.

Zombies of the Stratosphere (1952)

Director: Fred C. Brannon. **Cast:** Judd Holdren (Larry Martin), Aline Towne (Sue Davis), Wilson Wood (Bob Wilson), Lane Bradford (Marex), Stanley Waxman (Harding), John Crawford (Roth), Craig Kelly (Steele), Ray Boyle (Shane), Leonard Nimoy (Narab), Tom Steele (Truck Driver), Dale Van Sickel (Telegrapher), Roy Engel (Lawson), Jack Harden (Kerr), Paul Stader (Dock Heavy), Gayle Kellogg (Dick), Jack Shea (Policeman), Robert Garabedian (Elah).

Synopsis: Larry Martin (**Judd Holdren**), a leader in the Inter-Planetary Patrol, detects a rocketship coming to Earth. He takes to the air in his jet-powered flying suit and helmet to investigate and discovers Martian invaders, led by Marex (**Lane Bradford**). With Mars now orbiting too far away from the Sun, its ecology has been dying. The Martian invaders want to swap the orbital positions of Earth and Mars so that Mars will be closer to the Sun. They plan on achieving this by using hydrogen bomb plans stolen from Earth scientists to cause the two planets' orbits to swap positions. They will do so using specifically placed atomic explosions on both worlds. Martin also learns the Martians have Earth accomplices, the traitorous Dr. Harding (**Stanley Waxman**) and two gangsters, Roth (**John Crawford**) and Shane (**Ray Boyle**), who bedevil him and his associates, Sue Davis (**Aline Towne**) and Bob Wilson (**Wilson Wood**).

Locations: Iverson Movie Ranch, Vasquez Rocks, Stony Point, Chatsworth Train Depot, Topanga Canyon Blvd., a lot of stock footage, and Republic Studio front lot and backlot.

Larry Martin, Rocketman, flying over the hills with parts of Los Angeles in the valley below. Chapter 1.

Vasquez Rocks.

The zombies arrive.

All three images are from Chapter 1.

ZOMBIES OF THE STRATOSPHERE

Iverson Movie Ranch.
Chapter 1.

Santa Susanna Pass Road.
Chapter 8.

Unidentified location.
Chapter 8.

The Mansion Backlot Set.

Leaving Valleyheart Drive...
Chapter 1.

Preparing to enter the back gate to Republic Studio backlot.
Chapter 1.

Entering the back lot from Radford Avenue through the stylized gates and arriving at The Mansion set.
Chapter 1.

ZOMBIES OF THE STRATOSPHERE

The Mansion Back Lot Set.
Chapter 2.

A back door to the Mansion.
Chapter 1.

Rocketman has arrived at the Mansion.
Chapter 11.

Stony Point.

When these shots were filmed, Stony Point was at the end of Topanga Canyon Blvd. where it turned onto Santa Susanna Road. Now, Topanga Canyon Blvd. has been extended northward just beyond the 118 Freeway.
Chapter 4.

Chapter 11.

Chapter 4.

ZOMBIES OF THE STRATOSPHERE

Topanga Canyon Blvd.
Chapter 8.

The truck driver left stranded in a field next to Topanga Canyon Road.
Chapter 8.

Escaping with the Rocketman aboard the truck.
Chapter 8.

NOTE: Topanga Canyon Blvd. in this section now curves around the hill on the west side. During filming years, the roadway curved around the east side of the hill.

Chatsworth Train Depot.

The north end. Santa Susanna Mountains in the background. Chapter 1.

Chapter 1.

Chapter 1.

After the tank leaves the train depot, the rest of the sequence with the tank is stock footage.

Republic Studio Backlot.

New York Street.
Chapter 5.

The Alley between Western Street to the left and New York Square to the right.
Chapter 5.

Reverse view of the alley. To the rear there is a truck partially blocking the one-story Car Port building and Stage 4 beyond it.
Chapter 5.

Republic Studio Backlot.

New York Street.
Chapter 5.

Heading towards Western Street from the Miniature Pool.
The two story building with a doorway and windows, hides the cave sets in a large building almost the size of the Sky Cyclorama.
Chapter 2.

Closer look of the previous image. The entrance to the cave set building is now out of frame. The two "buildings" facing the camera are false fronts moved into place to hide the Hacienda Square behind it.
Chapter 3.

Republic Studio Backlot.

Miniature Pool.
Chapter 2.

Republic Studio Front Lot.

The Writer's Building.
Chapter 1.

The Property Department loading platform.
Chapter 8.

Above: Larry Martin fighting the robot on the cave set.
Below: Larry Martin taking off.

Jungle Drums of Africa
(1952)

Director: Fred C. Brannon. **Cast:** Clay Moore (Alan King), Phyllis Coates (Carol Bryant), Johnny Spencer (Bert Hadley), Roy Glenn (Naganto), John Cason (Regas), Henry Rowland (Kurgan), Steve Mitchell (Gauss), Don Blackman (Ebola), Felix Nelson (Nodala), Joel Fluellen (Matambo), Bill Washington (Tembo), Tom Steele (Constable 3), Robert Davis (Native 1), Roy Engel (Constable 1), Bob Johnson (Native 2).

Synopsis: Alan King (**Clayton Moore**) and his assistant, Bert Hadley (**Johnny Spencer**), arrive in Africa to develop uranium mining properties on tribal land of native chief Douanga (**Bill Walker**). They meet Regas (**John Cason**), foreign agent, but do not suspect him until he sabotages their jeep. They are menaced by animals, and attacked by natives acting under Regas' orders. They are rescued by Carol Bryant (**Phyllis Coates**), whose late father was a missionary with Douanga's tribe.

Locations: Iverson Movie Ranch, Burro Flats, and Republic Studio backlot.

Republic Studio Back Lot Jungle Area. Chapter 1.

Iverson Movie Ranch.

All three images.

Chapter 6.

Chapter 6.

Chapter 8.

Burro Flats.
Chapter 1.

Burro Flats.
Chapter 1.

Burro Flats.
Chapter 1.

Burro Flats.
Chapter 6.

Burro Flats.
Chapter 6.

Burro Flats.
Chapter 7.

JUNGLE DRUMS OF AFRICA

Republic Studio Backlot.

Cantina Street.
Chapter 1.

Brazos Street.
Chapter 1.

Brazos Street.
Chapter 1.

Republic Studio Backlot.

Native Village.
Chapter 12.

Lagoon and Cliffs.
Chapter 8.

Cave Set.
Chapter 6.

Canadian Mounties vs. Atomic Invaders (1953)

Director: Franklin Adreon. **Cast:** Bill Henry (Don Roberts), Susan Morrow (Kay Conway), Arthur Space (Marlof), Dale Van Sickel (Beck), Pierre Watkin (Morrison), Mike Ragan (Reed), Stanley Andrews (Anderson), Harry Lauter (Clark), Hank Patterson (Jed Larson), Edmund Cobb (Warner), Gayle Kellogg (Guy Sanders), Tom Steele (Mac), Jean Wright (Betty Warner).

Synopsis: A foreign power, which is represented by their agent Marlof (**Arthur Space**), attempts to set up secret missile bases in Canada to target the United States for their planned summer invasion. Meanwhile, acting on intelligence following the smashing of a spy ring in Montreal, Royal Canadian Mounted Police (RCMP) officers Don Roberts (**Bill Henry**) and Kay Conway (**Susan Morrow**) go undercover in a settling party headed for the Yukon. Marlof also has agents, Beck (**Dale Van Sickel**) and Reed (**Mike Ragan**), in the party en route to the site of the planned missile bases.

Locations: Big Bear and Republic Studio backlot.

Boulder Bay at Big Bear Lake. Chapter 9.

Big Bear Lake and Big Bear.

Chapter 9.

Chapter 9.

Chapter 5.

Republic Studio Back Lot.
Lagoon.
Chapter 9.

Republic Studio Back Lot.
Lagoon.
Chapter 9.

Chapter 9.

Republic Studio Backlot.

Brazos Street.
Chapter 9.

Cliff Cave.
Chapter 2.

Brazos Street.
Chapter 1.

Trader Tom of the China Seas
(1954)

Director: Franklin Adreon. **Cast:** Harry Lauter (Tom Rogers), Aline Towne (Vivian Wells), Lyle Talbot (Barent), Robert Shayne (Conroy), Fred Graham (Kurt Daley), Richard Reeves (Rebel Chief), Tom Steele (Gursan), John Crawford (Bill Gaines), Dale Van Sickel (Native Ambusher), Victor Sen Yung (Wang), Jan Arvan (Khan), Ramsey Hill (British Colonel), George Selk (Ole).

Synopsis: Tom Rogers (**Harry Lauter**), island trader, learns foreign agents are smuggling arms and munitions into a country under United Nations' protectorate and encouraging subversive native groups to revolt. He volunteers to help and begins a search for missing United Nations doctor and his daughter, Vivian Wells (**Aline Towne**).

Locations: Leo Carillo Beach, Iverson Movie Ranch, and Republic Studio backlot.

Republic Studio Back Lot Cave Set. Chapter 5.

Iverson Movie Ranch.

Chapter 9.

Chapter 9.

Chapter 9.

Leo Carillo State Beach,
35000 Pacific Coast Hwy,
Malibu.

Chapter 1.

Chapter 1.

Chapter 4.

Leo Carillo State Beach,
35000 Pacific Coast Hwy,
Malibu.

Chapter 5.

Chapter 5.

Chapter 5.

TRADER TOM OF THE CHINA SEAS

Republic Studio Back Lot.
Lagoon.
Chapter 1.

Republic Studio Back Lot.
Lagoon.
Chapter 6.

Republic Studio Back Lot.
Lagoon.
Chapter 1.

Republic Studio Backlot.

Spanish Street.
Chapter 9.

Near Western Street.
Chapter 3.

Identified as "ice rink" on a studio map, this was actually a cooler machine which supplied cold air to the buildings.
Chapter 6.

Man With the Steel Whip
(1954)

Director: Franklin Adreon. **Cast:** Richard Simmons (Jerry Randall), Barbara Bestar (Nancy Cooper), Dale Van Sickel (Crane), Mauritz Hugo (Barnett), Lane Bradford (Tosco), Pat Hogan (Chief), Roy Barcroft (Sheriff), Stuart Randall (Harris), Edmund Cobb (Lee), I. Stanford Jolley (Sloane), Guy Teague (Price), Alan Wells (Quivar), Tom Steele (Gage).

Synopsis: The ranchers of a western community are incensed by the growing number of Indian raids. They are ready to organize a posse to drive them off their reservation but Jerry Randall (**Richard Simmons**) manages to calm them. The local saloon keeper, Barnett (**Mauritz Hugo**), is eager to get the Indian land and is responsible for staging the Indian raids. Randall assumes the character of El Latigo, a hero from Indian legends and thereby gains the confidence of some of the tribe.

Locations: Iverson Movie Ranch, and Republic Studio backlot.

Republic Studio Back Lot lower section near the Duchess Ranch.
Chapter 3.

Iverson Movie Ranch.

Chapter 1.

Chapter 1.

Chapter 4.

Republic Studio Back Lot.
Dakota Street.
Chapter 1.

Republic Studio Back Lot.
Western Street.
Chapter 2.

Republic Studio Back Lot.
Duchess Ranch.
Chapter 1.

Republic Studio Backlot.

Running from Cantina Street, through Western Street, to the beginning of New York Street.
Chapter 3.

Cliffs and Caves Set.
Chapter 4.

Duchess Ranch.
Chapter 5.

Panther Girl of the Kongo (1955)

Director: Franklin Adreon. **Cast:** Phyllis Coates (Jean Evans), Myron Healey (Larry Sanders), Arthur Space (Morgan), John Day (Cass), Mike Ragan (Rand), Morris Buchanan (Tembu), Roy Glenn Sr. (Danka), Archie Savage (Ituri), Ramsay Hill (Stanton), Nasman Brown (Orlo), Dan Ferniel (Ebu), James Logan (Harris).

Synopsis: A scientist, Dr. Morgan (**Arthur Space**), develops a giant claw monster, which he uses to frighten natives away from his illegal diamond mine. The "Panther Girl" Jean Evans (**Phyllis Coates**), discovers the monster while she is engaged in photographing wild animals. In order to track down the beast, she enlists the aid of big game hunter Larry Sanders (**Myron Healey**). They start on the hunt and are attacked by hostile natives.

Locations: Lake Sherwood and Sherwood Forest, Corriganville, and Republic Studio backlot.

Sherwood Forest. Chapter 1.

Corriganville Movie Ranch.

Chapter 6.

Chapter 6.

Chapter 11.

PANTHER GIRL OF THE KONGO

Lake Sherwood.
Chapter 3.

Lake Sherwood.
Chapter 3.

Lake Sherwood.
Chapter 3.

Republic Studio Backlot.

Chapter 1.

Native Village.
Chapter 1.

Spanish Street.
Chapter 1.

Republic Studio Backlot.

Lagoon.
Chapter 9.

Lagoon.
Chapter 6.

Cliffs and Cave Sets.
Chapter 5.

King of the Carnival
(1955)

Director: Franklin Adreon. **Cast:** Harry Lauter (Bert King), Fran Bennett (June Edwards), Keith Richards (Daley), Robert Shayne (Jess Carter), Gregory Gay (Zorn), Rick Vallin (Art Kerr), Robert Clarke (Jim Hayes), Terry Frost (Travis), Mauritz Hugo (Sam), Lee Roberts (Hank), Chris Mitchell (Bill), Stuart Whitman (Mac), Tom Steele (Matt Winston), George DeNormand (Garth).

Synopsis: Treasury agents Art Kerr (**Rick Vallin**) and Jim Haynes (**Robert Clarke**) are investigating a global counterfeiting operation believed to be linked to the circus. Acrobat Bert King (**Harry Lauter**) agrees to help his old friend Art search for the counterfeiters, and his acrobatic partner, June Edwards (**Fran Bennett**), assists him. They are repeatedly threatened by two thugs, Daley (**Keith Richards**) and Travis (**Terry Frost**).

Locations: Leo Carillo Beach, Republic Studio front lot and backlot.

Republic Studio Back Lot Cave Sets.
Chapter 1.

Leo Carillo Beach.

Chapter 6.

Chapter 6.

Chapter 2.

Republic Studio Front Lot.

Transportation Department. In the background is Stage 12 with a view of the south end which was used by the Music and Accounting Departments. Chapter 8.

Republic Studio Back Lot.

The Cliffs and Caves outdoor sets. Chapter 9.

The Underwater Tank. Chapter 1.

Republic Studio Back Lot.
New England Street.
Chapter 9.

Republic Studio Back Lot.
New England Street.
Chapter 9.

Republic Studio Back Lot.
New England Street.
Chapter 7.

Republic Studio Back Lot.

Roadway from the Main Lot down to the lower Back Lot.
Chapter 4.

Republic Studio Back Lot.
Lower Back Lot roadway running below the upper Main Lot. The Cooling apparatus is in the upper left corner. The apartments across the street from the lot have been replaced with newer and taller ones.
Chapter 4.

Reverse shot of the Lower Back Lot raodway. You can barely see the stairway leading up. To the left of them, out of frame, is the Duchess Ranch.
Chapter 4.

Republic Studio Back Lot.

The Duchess Ranch House West End. Chapter 5.

The Duchess Ranch House East End. Chapter 6.

Duchess Ranch Barn and a little view of Studio City to the north. Chapter 4.

Commando Cody, Sky Marshal of the Universe (1953/1955)

Directors: Harry Keller, Franklin Adreon, and Fred C. Brannon. **Cast:** Judd Holdren (Commando Cody), Aline Towne (Joan Gilbert), William Schallert (Ted Richards), Peter Brocco (Dr. Varney), Craig Kelly (Commissioner Henderson), Gregory Gaye (The Ruler), Zon Murray (Ross), Stanley Waxman (Lenato), I. Stanford Jolley (Hardy), Richard Crane (Dick Preston), Lyle Talbot (Henchman Baylor), John Crawford (Alien), Mauritz Hugo (Henchman Mason), Joanne Jordan (The Queen of Mercury), Gloria Pall (The Moon Girl), Dale Van Sickel (Clancy), Lyle Talbot (Baylor), Eddie Foster (Mason), William Henry (Tantor), Kenneth MacDonald (Dispenser Station Superintendent), Rick Vallin (Capt. Duron), Sydney Mason (Capt. Ingor).

Synopsis: Dangerous weather and climate changes are ravaging the Earth. Masked super-scientist Commando Cody (**Judd Holdren**) is approached by the U.S. government to investigate. Among the tools at his disposal are a sonic-powered one-man flying suit with an aerodynamic helmet and a new Cody-designed and built rocket ship. With his colleagues Joan Gilbert (**Aline Towne**) and Ted Richards (**William Schallert**/chapters 1-3), later replaced by Dick Preston (**Richard Crane**/chapters 4-12), he ascertains the disasters are being caused by space-alien forces led by a mysterious "Ruler" (**Gregory Gaye**) of unknown planetary origins, with occasional help from hired, Earth-born criminals. Warding off various dangers, Cody and his associates are able to methodically close in on the culprits and reveal that The Ruler is from our sister world, Venus.

Locations: Radford Avenue Bridge, a lot of stock footage, and, Republic Studio front lot and backlot.

This serial was originally planned on being the first television series from Republic Pictures subsidiary, Hollywood Television Service. A full season of 39 Chapters was planned, but after filming the first three from February 25 to March 5, 1952, the project was put on hold because of union contract problems from both the actor's union and the soundtrack union. So, instead of a television series, it was decided to film only 12 complete Chapters at 30 minutes each and release them weekly (the first 3 were lengthened from their 27 min. 30 sec. lengths). The final 9 Chapters were filmed in January 1953. Actor William Schallert was lost to the series because of other commitments and Richard Crane replaced him (as a different character). By 1955, the union contract issues were finished and the 12 Chapters were released to television.

The serial was the way that the silent serials were first done—no cliffhangers at the end of each Chapter.

Republic Studio Front Lot.

The Writer's Building.
Chapter 1.

Adminstration Building on the right.
Chapter 1.

The grassy area between the southern fence and the Writer's Building. The building in the background, diagonally situated, was Herbert J. Yates' office.
Chapter 7.

Republic Studio Back Lot.

Western Street.
Chapter 1.

Republic Studio Back Lot.

Western Street.
Chapter 1.

Melody Ranch Barn.
Chapter 1.

Republic Studio Back Lot.
Cave Set
Chapter 3.

Republic Studio Back Lot.
New England Street.
Chapter 5.

Cliffs.
Chapter 7.

Republic Studio Back Lot.

Atop of the Cliffs.
Chapter 5.

Republic Studio Back Lot.
Caves Set redressed for snow.
Chapter 10.

Republic Studio Back Lot.
Caves Set redressed for snow.
Chapter 10.

Republic Studio Back Lot.

The roadway between the upper main lot and the lower back lot, passing the Cliffs set. Chapter 5.

Driving past the west side of the Cliffs set heading toward the Los Angeles River.. Chapter 9.

The roadway between the upper main lot and the lower back lot, passing the Cliffs set. Chapter 9.

TO THE READER

TO THE reading lover, an interesting, entertaining book is a bargain at any price—their problem being one of finding the right book to suit their personal taste—the kind of story that offers the most reading enjoyment.

Variety is essential to reading pleasure. And the publishers of **CP ENTERTAINMENT BOOKS** make every effort to provide the widest possible selection for the discriminating reader.

Under the **CP ENTERTAINMENT BOOKS** imprint appear biographies, pop culture, art, photography, genealogy, mystic, religion, reference, and performing arts—entertaining escape from the everyday world.

You will always find your greatest reading satisfaction under the distinctive imprint of **CP ENTERTAINMENT BOOKS**.

Find the **CP Entertainment Books** online at:

www.FictionHousePress.com

www.ingramcontent.com/pod-product-compliance
Lightning Source LLC
Chambersburg PA
CBHW081755300426
44116CB00014B/2126